THE BOOK OF
LAGOM

THE SWEDISH WAY OF LIVING JUST RIGHT

ISBN 978-91-1-308463-3
© Göran Everdahl & Norstedts, Stockholm 2018
Translated by Anna Holmwood
Design and illustrations: Lotta Kühlhorn & Söner
Cover design: Lotta Kühlhorn & Söner
Editors: Johan Andreasson and Jenny Lindblad
Proofreader: Ken Schubert
Photo Credits: see p. 188
Prepress: JK Morris AB, Värnamo
Printed in the EU 2019
Fourth printing

www.norstedts.se

*

Norstedts is a division of Norstedts Förlagsgrupp AB
Founded in 1823

GÖRAN EVERDAHL

THE BOOK OF LAGOM

THE SWEDISH WAY
OF LIVING JUST RIGHT

Translated by Anna Holmwood

NORSTEDTS

sort my waste.

Cardboard, aluminium cans, plastic, glass, metal and then the rest – household waste – they all go into their own separate space-guzzling containers, six of them, in one small kitchen. In one small flat.

Recycling takes time and space. I have to lug it three blocks, and when I get there, the dumpsters are invariably overflowing and stink. Then I have to unpack them all again. I do this gladly. For me and other Swedes, this is a lagom effort worth making for the sake of the environment.

Lagom is important, as best illustrated by a saying that every Swede knows by heart, one almost so lagom in length that it feels like a parody: "Lagom is best."

On first impression, it reads like one of those aggressively simple slogans dreamed up by a couple of overpaid copywriters at a hip advertising agency, or perhaps even a bilious piece of political propaganda. But appearances can be deceptive. The superlative "best" in this case is actually a rally cry for moderation.

Lagom, one of the few Swedish words without a direct equivalent in other languages (like smorgasbord and ombudsman), is usually translated as "not too little and not too much". And that would be correct. But in practice, the word is almost always used as a stand against excess.

"Lagom is best" often just means STOP. No more wine for you, that's quite enough tinsel in the Christmas tree thank you very much and sorry, that particular model of car is just too thirsty for gas. Lagom is best!

But it works the other way around too. Lagom doesn't mean a life of dinner without that glass of red, a bare Christmas tree or transport only by bike. That would be excessive after all. Again, *lagom is best*.

The lagom principle can also make life more beautiful. A practical example: the Rococo style was all the rage in eighteenth century Europe, with its epicentre in the Versailles hall of mirrors on the outskirts of Paris. Acres of gilding, tons of crystal, marble even in the lavatory.

But to get bling you need dough, and the Swedish aristocracy were of moderate means, at least compared to French kings. The result being that palaces and estates up and down the country opted for budget Rococo instead. Painted marble instead of the real deal, a pared down pomposity with fewer flourishes.

Slimmed-down glamour is still glamour, however. And when stripped of most of its decoration, the design suddenly comes to the fore. A lagom amount of gold leaf is still gold leaf. A bit of tasteful cheating, done well, can be tasteful and look great.

So what started as a necessity became an independent style known today as Swedish new classicism. To many, this look is easier on the eye than the voluptuous, exaggerated interiors of Versailles or the Hermitage in St Petersburg. Again: lagom is best.

In Sweden, we have a conflicted relationship to lagom. We joke about the "Land of Lagom" where no one dares stick out.

But to be consciously lagom, to go your own way when it

comes to career, clothes, travel and food – to allow yourself some luxuries, hopefully without harming the environment too much, that too is a way of being lagom. All sensible and kind, but also essential considering the world's scarce resources. It's better for us, and the planet, if we consume lagom.

There is something very reasonable about lagom. Sustainable, even. Lagom means wit that doesn't wound, warmth that doesn't dry out and fresh air without rough winds.

To put it another way: Lagom is a kind of individual lifestyle thermostat. Everyone is different. There is no ideal level of lagom; it varies from person to person and place to place.

And yet, there is something exhilarating about the search for your own ideal conditions – to find your own personal Lagom. It might not be perfect (perfection is pretty much the opposite of lagom), but a life that maintains that messy balance between work and home, gravity and joy, rest and action, can't possibly be bad. If nothing else, it can be perfectly comfortable.

And that's when lagom is really best.

Contents

CHAPTER 1

THE HISTORY OF
THE LAND
OF LAGOM

Sweden is a Scandinavian country with an area of 407 000 square kilometres and 10 million inhabitants. The capital, Stockholm, is also the country's largest city, followed by Gothenburg and Malmö.

Sweden is a monarchy but the King, Carl XVI Gustaf, only has a representative function. Laws are drawn up in parliament and the country is run by the government, which over the last few decades has alternated between the left- and right-wing blocs.

Average life expectancy is 80 for Swedish men and 84 for women. 15% of Swedes live rurally and 9 out of 10 citizens use the Internet.

The average Swede drinks 3.4 cups of coffee a day, which is the second highest in the world, after our caffeine-addict neighbours the Finns.

The History of the Land of Lagom

My old friend Alexander's father is Greek and his mother is Swedish. After retiring, his parents started spending their summers in Stockholm and the rest of the year on Crete. Over time they seemed to switch nationalities. His mother soon adapted to the Mediterranean lifestyle, eating late and driving fast. His father, on the other hand, prefers living in a place where you know both workmen and your state pension will arrive on time. Or indeed, that the state pension exists at all.

Reliability and stability aren't sexy, of course. Spontaneity and unpredictability are more exciting, sensual even. And yet Swedes have an almost fetishistic relationship to dependable timetables and health recommendations. Phrases like "functioning health insurance" make our eyes mist over and our breath quicken.

But that sort of peculiar penchant doesn't become part of an entire culture overnight. For centuries, Swedes have, rightly and occasionally wrongly, put their faith in society as a whole to function. This applies to everything from automatic invitations for breast screenings – which save lives – to everyday problems like clearing snow, which can be a touchy subject if you live close to the Artic Circle.

Perhaps Swedes discovered this passion for the predictable in the seventeenth century with Count Axel Oxenstierna. He was

Chancellor for two famous monarchs: the war king Gustavus Adolphus and his wayward daughter Queen Christina (played on screen by both Greta Garbo and Liv Ullman). But from our lagom historical perspective, Oxenstierna is most interesting for being a freakishly effective super-bureaucrat.

Oxenstierna reportedly told his son, the diplomat Gustaf: "If you only knew just how little sense rules the fate of the world."

"Nowadays there are 'latte pappas' in Stockholm, young men who park their buggies outside the city's cafés and spend all day slurping and chatting with their friends. Not that the time off is necessarily split evenly, and the fathers seem to often take theirs to coincide with the winter Olympics or football's World Cup."

With that attitude to the ruling class, there could be only one thing on his mind: damage control. To construct a society as immune as possible to whim, corruption and external shocks. Oxenstierna certainly wasn't lazy: he improved the education system, standardised government for the entire nation and founded the postal service.

AXEL OXENSTIERNA
Målning av S P Tilmann
Foto SPA

Drottning Kristina.

The great Swedish empire soon collapsed, but Oxenstierna's reforms remained in place. "The state's cake is small but sure." A seemingly ancient Swedish saying could now be put into practice.

Not that everyone was equal under the law; Count O made sure the noblemen kept their privileges. But a hundred years later, in 1766, Sweden got the world's first act of parliament guaranteeing freedom of the press and in 1842, compulsory elementary education was brought in, giving everyone both the right and the duty to learn to read and write.

There it was, the cornerstone of the term lagom: justice. Pay your taxes and never jump a queue; these are almost sacred principles in Sweden. Even self-proclaimed open-minded, liberal Swedes start ranting and raving over the lack of queuing in the rest of Europe.

Per Albin Hansson

The worst scolding I ever got was when I mistakenly jumped a taxi queue. And in 1984, my mother nearly died of shame when she found herself on the same bus as Prime Minister Olof Palme – Swedish PMs take the bus of course! – and it looked as if she boarded without paying. The bus was crowded and she had to step down at a stop to let another passenger off. Palme didn't see her step down, only come back on again, without paying. And so he gave her a dirty look. The horror.

Palme's folksiness wasn't confined to bus rides. He lived with his family in a simple terraced house on the outskirts of Stockholm and his telephone number was listed in the directory under P, so that every citizen could reach him. His wife and children were readily harassed, but still, so democratic.

These days it would be unthinkable for a politician to be forced to resign for something as humdrum as an affair, but try to reduce your tax bill through entirely legal means, or worse, don't pay your television license? Then it's full moral panic. Thank you and goodbye, Minister!

Fairness is an emotional subject in a country where paternal leave has for many years been part of the social insurance system. Nowadays there are "latte pappas" in Stockholm, young men who park their buggies outside the city's cafés and spend all day slurping and chatting with their friends. Not that the time off is necessarily split evenly, and the fathers seem to often take theirs to coincide with the winter Olympics or football's World Cup.

The idea of fairness has been around for a long time, but was strengthened in the twentieth century when Sweden was modernised during the long reign of the Social Democrats. After World War II, Sweden's reputation was that of model socialist state. The reality was of course more complex. Conflicts between political and economic interests arose in Sweden just as in the rest of the world.

But still … In 1938, the trade union confederation and the employers association signed the Saltsjöbaden Agreement, something we call "the labour market constitution", in which issues like the right to strike was regulated to the satisfaction of all – and without the state having to stick its nose in and legislate.

This was neither an American-style predatory capitalism nor a Soviet planned economy but something else, a collaboration: what would later be termed the "third way". Or what we mere mortals call lagom.

"The twentieth century still influences everything that is Swedish and lagom, from specialised government-owned alcohol shops to free healthcare for all. Secure, reliable – lagom."

Up until the 1980s, negotiations were often characterized by "the spirit of Saltsjöbaden", meaning a general willingness to work together. Not that these natural enemies, the unions and industry, lay together like the lion and the lamb in the Garden of Eden – but it kind of feels that way, at least compared to the harder attitudes of the present. The booming economy was probably a contributing factor to this harmony.

A couple of years before the Saltsjöbaden Agreement was

thrashed out, the Swedish prime minister, the fatherly Per Albin Hansson, started referring to the country as Folkhemmet (literally "the people's home"), a phrase which became equivalent to the Swedish welfare state. The idea was that society, and the state, was a home for everyone: "Nobody looks down on anyone else. No one tries to get advantage at the expense of anyone else, the strong don't hold down or plunder the weak. A good home is governed by equality, consideration, cooperation and mutual help."

When translated into English "the people's home" sounds vaguely Maoist, but it has a pleasant ring to Swedish ears – or at the least a reliable ring, in a nostalgic and old-fashioned kind of way. It reminds us of a time when everything, from dental care to the opera, was to be democratised and made available to all.

One result was the creation of municipal music colleges: high quality instruction in music available to all, even children whose parents couldn't afford expensive piano lessons. The consequences can still be felt today, with this endless factory line of pop stars and a nation obsessed with winning the Eurovision Song Contest.

Other outcomes were unpredictable and difficult to discern in retrospect. While high culture like opera and poetry spread to the people, folk and pop culture was demonised for decades, however undemocratic that turned out to be. ABBA, today a national treasure, was spat on in the culture supplements of the 1970s.

The Land of Lagom of today, in all its sensible and more absurd formations, is nevertheless a product of "the people's home" era of the 1900s – a troubled time for Europe as a whole, but comparatively calm in Sweden. We had the time and the means to drill down into the details.

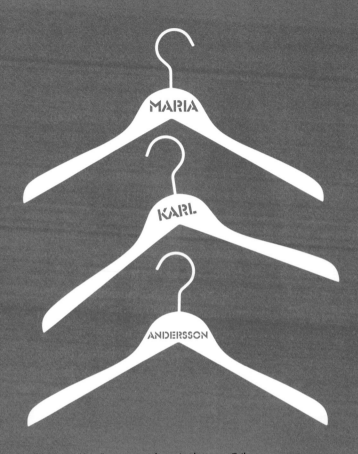

"Son" names such as Andersson, Eriksson etc continue to be widespread in Sweden, but even more surnames, 35% in fact, have meanings associated with nature, such as Lind ("Linden tree"), Björk ("Birch tree") and Berg ("Mountain").

On average per year, Swedes consume 346 bottles of premium strength beer (5% abv and above), or 92 bottles of wine, or 32 bottles of spirits. This amounts to 6.5 beers or 1.75 bottles of wine a week.

Wine is the most popular drink, followed by premium strength beer, spirits, "folk beer" (2.25% to 3.5% abv) and cider.

Wine consumption has increased by 9.5% in the last decade. Premium strength beer consumption went down by 8% and spirits by 30% between 2006 and 2016.

Lagom landmarks

1955 • INTRODUCTION OF THE GOVERNMENT MONOPOLY ON ALCOHOL

In the mid-1950s, alcohol rationing, which had been in place since 1914, finally came to an end. But to liberalise the sale of alcohol completely and thus risk widespread alcohol abuse? That was just too much for the Land of Lagom. The solution: a government monopoly on the sale of beer, wine and spirits through Systembolaget, which encourages low, or rather lagom, consumption.

Sometimes Systembolaget's propaganda against its own products has gone to absurd lengths. In the 1970s, full-page adverts were taken out that admonished the Swedes in all seriousness that no one could really drink like James Bond or the petty bourgeoisie depicted in the British TV hit *The Brothers*. Thanks for enlightening us, Systembolaget!

Debate over the years about whether the monopoly should stand has been spirited. Is it even legal, considering Sweden is part of the EU free-trade zone? And for many years, the shops were closed completely on weekends. Anyone who had run out at home was kindly directed to go to a bar.

Yet Swedes have an affection for their Systembolaget. Because paradoxically, the system means that every small town in Sweden has a first-rate wine selection – all Systembolagets must be made equal after all! There are those who claim that the average Systembolaget has a better selection than an exclusive wine shop on the Champs-Élyssée.

1956 • THE CURTSY STRIKE

Fresh from her coronation, Queen Elizabeth II made a state visit to Sweden and in the name of equality, parliamentary minister Ulla Lindström refused to curtsy. Instead, Lindström bowed just like her male colleagues – a perfectly lagom protest in contemporary eyes. But at the time, the Swedish and British press were enraged.

1958 • DONALD DUCK AND FRIENDS WISH YOU A MERRY CHRISTMAS

Sweden is one of the world's most secular countries, so of course our Christmas traditions must be suitably moderate. Bizarrely enough, the most beloved of which is a Disney cartoon. There is an explanation.

Cartoons were rarely broadcast on Swedish television in 1958, but this was the era in which the Donald Duck & Co comic sold in record numbers. When SVT broadcast a medley of Disney cartoons and clips on Christmas Eve that year, it became such a hit that they repeated it the following year, and the next and ...

These days 3 pm on Christmas Eve is called "Donald o'clock", and like all other holy rituals, every detail has to be just right. Any change is tantamount to a declaration of war. In 1982, a TV producer tried substituting the *Ferdinand the Bull* clip for *The Ugly Duckling,* causing a massive wave of protests — or as we say in Swedish, a folkstorm. Thankfully, Ferdinand was back on screen the following Christmas.

1965 • SELLING MELLANÖL IN SHOPS

Certain brands of beer began appearing in supermarkets during the 1960s and 1970s, an exception to the state monopoly of the Systembolaget. The beer was 4.5% in strength (as are many lagers) and was called mellanöl, "medium beer" – to distinguish it from the stronger 5% and above products, as well as those that contained nearly no alcohol at all, referred to as light. A classic lagom solution!

Unfortunately, mellanöl turned out to be not quite lagom enough in the long run: alcohol-related injuries among the young increased, and in 1977 Systembolaget reclaimed their lager monopoly. And just to make matters even more confusing, these days beers between 2.25% and 3.5% are sold in supermarkets under the name folköl, the "people's beer".

1967 • LANGUAGE REFORM

There is nothing more un-lagom than people being referred to by titles. So naturally, in the 1960s Swedes started addressing each other by first names and using the familiar "du" instead of the more formal "ni". "Doctor", "Sir" and "Miss" were seen as distancing, rude even. These days, even the Swedish King Carl XVI Gustaf is fighting a losing battle to be called "Your Majesty".

For the British, German and French, Mr/Mrs, Herr/Frau and Monsieur/ Madame are natural ways to address someone – but few Swedes since the 1970s have used the titles "herr" or "fru". Some young people in the service sector have tried to revive them in recent years, to the consternation of the older generation – mainly because these youngsters have no idea how or when to use them. It's not easy playing "class society" kids!

1974 • LÄTT & LAGOM MARGARINE

How do you make something as novel and strange as a sandwich spread with half the butter a hit among conservative, suspicious consumers? By giving it a reassuring name. Introduced in 1974, it contained only 40% fat and was called *Lätt & Lagom* ("Light & Lagom"). It flew off the shelves and continues to do so to this day.

In 1983, a competing margarine called simply *Lätta* ("Light"), was launched. The advertising campaign consisted of large posters with sweaty, ripped athletes looking straight into the camera and saying, "I've decided not to be fat." The newspapers deemed the campaign "fascist". Which of course is neither light nor lagom!

Donald Duck's dominance of Christmas on Channel 1 irritated the Swedes of the 1970s. Wasn't he the face of American capitalism? Didn't he have a notoriously bad temper and often resort to violence? Some of the clips were censored to make them fit better with the politics of the day, but this was still Disney. Something had to be done.

Not a problem. A charming Swedish Christmas cartoon was cobbled together for Channel 2. A friendly teenager gives out Christmas presents meant for the rich to homeless people and prostitutes. It has aired every Christmas since, just like Donald Duck. Capitalism on Channel 1, socialism on Channel 2, but never at the same time – everyone has to have a chance to see both. The mixed economy in a nutshell!

1976 • THE POMPERIPOSSA EFFECT

Astrid Lindgren, famous the world over for Pippi Longstocking books, was hit hard by the marginal tax rate of the mid-70s. So hard in fact, she had to pay 106% of her income to the state. This could not be deemed lagom even in Sweden, and Lindgren reacted by writing an op-ed article that read like a fairy tale for grown-ups about her alter-ego, the heavily-taxed witch Pomperipossa. The Social Democrats lost the general election the following year, the first time in four decades. Don't mess with Pippi's mum!

1980 • THE VOTE FOR LAGOM NUCLEAR POWER

After the Three Mile Island accident at Harrisburg, Pennsylvania in 1979, Swedish voters and politicians got cold feet. Were nuclear power stations on home turf really such a good idea? A referendum was held: expansion or closure, yes or no. Which side won? We're talking about Sweden here, so it goes without saying there was also a middle alternative.

Option 1: expansion, Option 2: gradual phasing out, and Option 3, the environmentally friendly one: immediate closure. Swedes voted for the lagom number 2, and the phasing out has been so extremely gradual that the nuclear power stations sputter on to this day.

1986 • VOILÀ: MELLANMJÖLK!

To many Swedes, a carton of milk will always be the ultimate symbol of lagom, a veritable monument to our national fixation with equality and compromise. Mellanmjölk ("medium milk") is not as rich as whole milk (3% fat), but neither as stingy as skimmed (at 0.5%). Coming in at a perfectly middling 1.5% mellanmjölk is... Say it with me folks: Lagom!

Originally launched with a different composition and the bureaucratic-sounding name "1% Milk", the people rose up and began calling it Mellanmjölk. The official name soon changed. You can't get anything more democratic than a drink named spontaneously by the consumers themselves. Considering how important milk is to the Swedish diet, it has to be considered luck of the tallest order that we also have one of the lowest levels of lactose intolerance in the world. We are milk freaks!

Swedes love to think that the assortment of rules known collectively as Allemansrätten ("Everyman's Right", but perhaps better translated as "The Right to Roam") is somehow unique and ancient, but strictly speaking it is neither. Versions of it have existed for a long time – but it became official only in the 1940s.

In practice, everyone has a right to roam all forest and land in Sweden, even when privately owned. Common in the rest of the world, "PRIVATE" signs are pretty much forbidden in Sweden. Everyone can walk, camp, swim, make a fire and pick berries and mushrooms, with only minimal restrictions, such as keeping out of sight of landowner dwellings. We have to be lagom about this after all!

The right to roam came into its modern form during "the people's home" period when Swedes started having longer holidays and moving around more. But it was only written into law in 1994: "Everyone should have equal access to nature."

1995 • THE CHOCOLATE SCANDAL

Swedish political scandals, unlike the British and American varieties, are rarely about sex. Not that Swedish politicians aren't unfaithful, it's just not a feature of our politicking. However, other taboos about appropriate behaviour for public servants apply. A big no-no: buying snacks on the taxpayer's dime.

It's hard not to sympathize with Mona Sahlin, the deputy prime minister who developed a love of imported chocolate so strong it proved to be her downfall. In fact, according to the newspaper Expressen, Sahlin used her government Eurocard to pay for "clothes, car rental, cash withdrawals – and two Toblerones." Sahlin had to resign as her messy private finances were exposed. A whopping 98 unpaid parking tickets and a trip to the Bahamas on public money were also uncovered, but today Swedish people remember only one thing: those damn bars of chocolate.

CHAPTER 2

10 KG

A LAGOM
LIFE

LAGOM EXERCISE

70% of Swedes exercise or play sport at least once a week, more than any other European country.

A Lagom Life

The story of Goldilocks and the Three Bears. Remember that one?

As entertainment for children, perhaps not as problematic as the one about Hansel and Gretel – two children burn an old woman to death in her house, lovely! – but it does glamourise burglary, let's at least be clear about that.

You have to wonder, is an entitled little girl who breaks into the home of three hardworking bears for kicks really a suitable role model for kids? Anyway. Once inside, Goldilocks doesn't just help herself to whatever she pleases, she delivers opinions on everything in sight as well. Strong opinions.

Oh no, the food is too cold. Or too hot. The bed is too hard, or much too soft. Goldilocks is so consumed by her critique she doesn't seem to give a second thought to the possibility that the world's largest land carnivore might just be on its way home. And yet, despite all odds, she finds both food and a place to rest that are just lagom.

That's certainly one way of reading Goldilocks, as the picky opinionator and taste terrorist.

But she could also be seen an individual on the lookout for solutions, someone without preconceptions who is prepared to compromise.

Both descriptions work, at least in part, for us Swedes. Yes, we can be mannered, tiresome even, in our search for practical solutions. A smug "This is how we do things in Sweden" is a phrase that visitors soon learn to recognize.

A century of nearly uninterrupted material prosperity has not made us less inclined to complain. But there is also a positive to the Goldilocks syndrome: historically, we've been pretty good at making sensible compromises.

"That's certainly one way of reading Goldilocks, as the picky opinionator and taste terrorist."

Consider the washing machine. Practical but expensive, not to mention bulky. A dilemma. What to do?

Swedes were already wrestling with this problem as early as the 1920s and 1930s, when the washing machine was a brand new invention. The Social Democratic concept of "the people's home" lauded technical innovation that gave Swedish women more free time. And yet, not all families could afford nor had the space for this metal contraption that, on top of everything else, had to be connected to the mains.

To wash, or not to wash. As existential queries go, perhaps not the most profound, but it needed an answer nevertheless. Did we really have to choose between investing in our own machine and schlepping our clothes all the way to a laundromat?

The solution: the communal washing room. Unusual out-

side of Sweden, it is in the basement of a block of purpose-built flats kitted out especially with a washing machine, space for drying and a mangle. The first was built in Stockholm in the 1920s and they are ubiquitous to this day, whether in rented or privately-owned blocks.

How about that for a solution: everyone gets access to a washing machine without having to own one. A perfect example of the magic of lagom, a miracle that's sorely needed in today's world.

"Even the subject of weight loss makes emotions run high; just look at the impassioned fights going on between adherents of diets such as low carbohydrate, high fat (LCHF) and the 5:2 Fast. Take a stand, pick a side!"

Our whole culture these days is geared towards a constant barrage of choices, sometimes between an almost never-ending number of alternatives – that's how it feels in the olive oil or toothpaste aisles anyway. But sometimes we are also asked to make a decision between two diametrical opposites. That ideology is too capitalist, that one too liberal, yuck and eugh.

Life is more turning into a fight between extremes. Right against left, eco-warriors against climate change deniers, East against West, Christian fundamentalists against Islamic fundamentalists. And in the line of fire, we poor souls trying our best not to get caught up in commentator battles, Twitter spats and Facebook bullying.

This polarisation isn't just ideological; it reaches into our psyches almost like a split-personality disorder. Take our private lives: you can strive for and achieve everything, both in the office and at home, but this only results in even harder choices between work and leisure. Even the subject of weight loss makes emotions run high; just look at the impassioned fights between adherents to diets such as the low carbohydrate and high fat (LCHF) and the 5:2 Fast. Take a stand, pick a side!

The common denominator in these issues: a desire for purity and an unwillingness to compromise. We live in anxious times, a little bit like the Reformation of the 1500s. Just as the new printing press spread fresh ideas at an unprecedented speed, we are bombarded daily with information and propaganda via the Internet.

"No, I don't need to eat perfectly, but it doesn't hurt to keep an eye on the calories. A lagom eye."

Times like these make extremists out of us all. The tone is raised to such a pitch that we have to scream just to be heard above the noise. And so slogans and insults naturally become the everyday. Personally, I happen to be a diet extremist of the yoyo kind. I've gone up and down by hundreds of kilos over the years, but always in units of five to ten. Gluttony interspersed with abstinence: not exactly healthy. Still, you can actually get a little wiser with time. I've managed to channel my inner Goldilocks and suppress some of my ambitions without dispensing with them completely. No, I don't need to eat perfectly, but it doesn't hurt to keep an eye on the calories. A lagom eye.

Which is to say, we could learn a lot from lagom thinking in times like these. A lot of the current opinion warfare is just unnecessary. Get up out of the trenches, you don't need to fight! Trust your own instincts and common sense and listen just enough to the unsolicited shouting matches.

We don't, for example, need to worship the same god in the same way, just as not everyone needs to own a washing machine. There are solutions enough to leave us all satisfied. Or at least equally dissatisfied: a realistic compromise that often works surprisingly well.

In the long run, this lagom thinking emphasises the brotherhood of man. Or should that be sisterhood? Hmm...

Liberty, equality, siblinghood! There you go, a lagom catchy slogan for the modern age.

The Swedish flag marks those particularly Swedish obsessions, things like what to eat for fika, top Ingmar Bergman films and suicide.

Lagom: A brief lifestyle guide

How much is too much, or too little, or the perfect amount of lagom? Enjoy a small selection of lagom judgments on some of the most divisive issues of our times.

Swedes love to travel – to the sun, to the snow, away for a weekend. We like to get out into the world, and often. 58% travel abroad at least once a year. Only 1% have never left the country.

Too much

Adventure holidays to remote and uninhabited islands, impenetrable jungles – why not? Still, there are limits. If you feel the urge to match the feats of the Frenchman Sylvain Dornon, who walked 2,900 kilometers from Paris to Moscow in 1891 on stilts, or Plennie L. Wingo who trekked 13,000 kilometers backwards from California to Turkey in 1931–1932, just calm down! Or, if you insist on covering long stretches in reverse, do as Wingo did and build yourself a pair of periscope goggles.

Too little

Package holidays and bus trips have their attractions, but surely we go abroad to see more than the inside of a bus and to speak with people who come from other countries? Try venturing out without your guide, it's fun!

Lagom!

Swedes who can afford it often complement package holidays with a weekend city break a little closer to home. A short trip that doesn't require too many days. A night in Helsinki could also be an adventure.

In Sweden we have our own expression for Danish hygge, "mys". It means the exact same thing: a cozy atmosphere, preferably with dim lighting.

Too much

Nowadays it seems, "hygge" has turned into a competitive sport. Magazines and weekend supplements print endless trend features and "rules for hygge". How many cushions and blankets does one person have to put up with? Where to draw the line in all this hygge madnesss is of course up to the individual. Me, I draw it at incense. A steaming loaf of freshly baked bread? Yes, please. Columns of incense clouding my room? No, a thousand times no!

Too little

Since we live cloaked in polar darkness for half the year, we Swedes have strong opinions on lighting. We are drawn to gentle spotlights, but also candlelight. But there is one rule that trumps all others: no fluorescent lamps. EVER. A lonely, naked bulb without a shade or even worse, a strip of fluorescent lighting, is considered the blasphemous work of a shameless mys-wrecker.

Lagom!

In Sweden, mys or hygge is strongly linked to Friday night, the end of the working week and a time to exhale. Pillows and blankets are optional, but snacks are a must. Cheese and nuts are all good, but nothing beats crisps.

Swedes average over two kilos of crisps per year, and 70% of those are gobbled down between Thursday and Saturday. Popular flavours include: chives & dill and sourcream & onion.

Sweden's most legendary filmmaker Ingmar Bergman (1918–2007) is well known all over the world for his melancholy. There is more to his films than angst, but don't overdose in the beginning!

Too much

Bergman's *Persona* from 1966 – a collection of tightly composed black and white tableaux in which Bibi Andersson and Liv Ullman might at any moment merge into a single person – is Bergman at his most undiluted and abstract. And much like a shot of straight snaps, not for everyone.

Too little

All These Women (1964) was Bergman's first colour film and also a sex comedy. Bergman was in unchartered territory and this is as un-Bergman as it gets. Apart from *The Serpent's Egg* (1977), a Cabaret pastiche with hints of gothic horror – one of which is Liv Ullman singing.

Lagom!

Fanny and Alexander (1982) is perfect for the novice, a tasting menu of all Bergman's favorite motifs if you will, such as the brevity of life, bad fathers, the magic of the theatre, symbolic dream scenes – and fart jokes!

Everybody needs to keep in shape but most of us are just too lazy. And then we feel guilty. And then we console ourselves with chocolate. Shouldn't we just console ourselves with an all-out workout? Probably.

Too much

Kettlebells are those cast iron bells that strong men in amusement parks used to lift to excite the crowds. A little bit like a cannonball with a handle. Now popular among exercise nuts, they are effective to be sure. But to the ordinary amateur they look frightening. We're talking full-on strongman horror.

Too little

At the other end of the spectrum, we have golf. Regardless what we think about him, it must be said that US President Donald Trump has some very interesting theories about cardiovascular activity. He claims that we all have a limited amount of energy, like a battery, and that it should be preserved at all costs – all physical effort is harmful. So the Donald's sport of choice is golf. Which he plays incessantly. And so he has the physique of... Donald Trump.

Lagom!

Dog owners are in better-than-average shape for the simple reason that they are forced to take daily walks. According to new findings, a 30-minute walk only four times a week can prevent Alzheimer's in old age and alleviate existing symptoms.

Hard cash is an area where the Swedes are actually extreme. Sweden is on its way to becoming the world's first cashless society, to the extent that ATMs are now so rare in Stockholm that they are almost tourist attractions.

Too much

For those with a working knowledge of economics and computers, the digital currency Bitcoin could be worth investing in. To the rest of us? Risky, difficult to understand, even harder to value. We'll pass on that one for now.

Too little

Nowadays I can go for weeks without seeing a single banknote or coin. My credit card, however, is burning hot. Small amounts between friends can be exchanged with a smartphone app. This is convenient, but also a little sterile. Handling physical money today is an exercise in nostalgia. It makes me feel like I'm playing Monopoly.

Lagom!

Cash is an invention that has stood the test of time. The earliest coins were created over 2,500 years ago and looked pretty much like the ones we use today. Of course, as technology goes, they have their disadvantages: coins and banknotes are easy to steal, lose or counterfeit. But using and exchanging cash is usually easy and risk-free. Simply put, cash works.

What constitutes a lagom amount of time spent on social media is, of course, a matter of personal preference. A bit like how many times a week it's okay to have a drink or two before your evening meal. Social media can be addictive – some people feel the urge to check their feeds several times a minute: Facebook-aholics!

Too much

It's not unusual for one person to have active accounts on Facebook, Instagram, Twitter, Snapchat and LinkedIn. At the same time. Seriously, LinkedIn? Isn't that just another name for spam? If notifications for all these services were turned on, your phone would sound like a round-the-clock fire alarm. Bow down to your new master, the smartphone!

Too little

The "Digital Detox", as in time spent away from the web, is a modern term and interesting, not least because the actual wording seems to assume that social media are poisonous. It's addictive, obviously. But only the mentally robust can pull off a digital detox, because it means not knowing how many people liked that picture of the misshapen potato their friend up-loaded yesterday... Life is a struggle, indeed.

Lagom!

You can actually limit yourself to one or maybe two news feeds. Stub out Twitter and see how much happier the whole world suddenly feels! Definitely less angry. Personally, I let Facebook notify me when my ten closest friends upload a picture or update their status. I don't have to surf endless waves of information, but I have a lagom sense of what is going on.

A controversial question: why do more Swedes take their own lives than those of other nations? Because we do, don't we? As it happens, no.

Too much

As everyone knows, Sweden has the highest rate of suicide per capita in the world. Except that it's never been true. The source of this particular piece of fake news was a speech made by US President Eisenhower in Chicago in 1960. Swedes had been mentally weakened by a suffocating socialist welfare state, he claimed. Two years later, during a visit to Sweden, Eisenhower apologized and corrected himself, but this time his words didn't get quite the same reach. Today, the highest rates of suicide are in some of the former Soviet states of Eastern Europe, where alcoholism is widespread. In 2016, Lithuania topped the list of suicides per capita.

Too little

According to World Health Organization statistics, Sweden came in number 31 on the same list in 2017. But data collected in large parts of the world are far from reliable, as the social stigma attached to suicide means that authorities are often reluctant to list it as the cause of death.

Lagom!

Strictly speaking, the appropriate number of suicides in a country should be zero. However, it appears that while Scandinavians are usually considered a solemn bunch, they also usually top the UN's annual World Happiness Report. In 2017, the Norwegians were happiest, while Sweden ended up in ninth place. The USA came in at 14 and Rwanda was last at 151.

Trend-conscious Swedes have their finger on the pulse even when it comes to the latest in pet fashion. One year it's rats, the next it's chihuahuas in handbags. But what is the lagom pet?

Too much

Owning your own horse. A bit like having a washing machine: it all depends on having the space and the money. But washing machines don't need grooming and shoeing! Keeping a horse in your own stable, as opposed to someone else's, is a major undertaking.

Too little

Stick insects. Can this creature even be considered a companion? When a beloved pet can lie dead for several days without anyone noticing, maybe it's time to raise ambitions a little and at least get a turtle?

Lagom!

It's all a question of balance. Birds, dogs and fish all have their advantages – but the true lagom pet is the cat. Care is pretty much limited to emptying the litter tray; exercise the cat takes care of itself, often managing to combine it with the hunting of vermin. Why thank you.

The British brag about their quick-witted Jane Austen heroines such as Elizabeth Bennet in *Pride and Prejudice*, and the French have Zola's *Nana* and Flaubert's *Madame Bovary*. Swedish literary heroines may be fewer in number, but they can hold their own.

Too much

Lisbeth Salander, the punk hacker in Stieg Larsson's *Millennium* trilogy, is a global celebrity. She is certainly charismatic, and pretty extreme. How extreme? Let's just say that she's a world-class computer geek with a photographic memory who, if the situation demands it, is more than willing to burn people to death.

Too little

Elsalill in Nobel Prizewinner Selma Lagerlöf's *The Treasure* cuts an unusually grey figure. She falls in love with her sister's murderer, the crooked Scottish mercenary Sir Archie, and then she dies. Nice going, Elsalill...! If Lisbeth Salander had been in charge, Archie would have been a pile of ashes by page 30.

Lagom!

Astrid Lindgren's classic children's heroine Pippi Longstocking is not a victim like Elsalill, but neither is she a murderous maniac like Lisbeth. No, she's a strong, independent young child with, as the song from the old Pippi movie goes, "a monkey, horse and house." Which is about everything anyone needs in life really.

Yet another beloved Swedish word, fika. That is, an afternoon snack break. Traditionally this consists of coffee and something sweet like a cinnamon bun or a biscuit. Until the 1950s, no self-respecting host served up less than seven different types of baked goods to their guests. That kind of excess is rare these days. And Swedes have better teeth as a result.

Too much

American baking culture with its gargantuan muffins and cookies the size of bowling balls has invaded most of the world. Swedes hesitated at first: one cookie corresponded to four or five Swedish biscuits. But once the shock wore off, we too bit from the poisoned apple. With extra frosting.

Too little

Of course, health-conscious people eat snacks that can be both delicious and satisfying. But they can also consist of wishy-washy powder-based protein drinks, or quark. Don't know what quark is? Congratulations. I mean, there's nothing wrong with quark. Apart from the taste.

Lagom!

There is something quite wonderful about a simple fika. A cup of coffee and some afternoon conversation is exactly what you need to make it through to evening. And a traditional Swedish biscuit never goes amiss. Or two; they're quite small!

CHAPTER 3

LAGOM
UNIQUE

Finnish and Arabic are the most spoken languages in Sweden after Swedish. Persian, Polish and Somalian are also on the rise.

Lagom Unique

How many words inspire actual legends? Not a lot. Only a few rare expressions stand out against the dull grey of the everyday. By lucky coincidence, lagom happens to be one of them.

The story of the word's origins is straightforward enough. It is an ancient, exotic tale that is related to this day as gospel truth. According to this lagom creation myth, the word came about during the Viking era, sometime between 800 and 1000 A.D. A mug of mead was passed around the fire and the Norsemen would remind each other to drink "lagom", from the phrase "laget runt", literally "around the band." Everyone got their share.

And why not? It's a nice thought, everyone from Harald Hardrade, Sweyn Forkbeard, Ragnar Lodbrok and little Rollo who went on to rule Normandy, the whole rabble-rousing gang all waiting patiently for their turn, safe in the knowledge they would get their rightful share of the available intoxicants before starting on their next rampage. Cheers and thank you!

It's a lovely image that fits perfectly with modern Swedish understanding of polite and appropriate behaviour, as well as our sense of social and economic fairness. Unfortunately it's also completely made up. It would be just as true to say that our seafaring ancestors liked to relax with a lagom mug of 3.5% abv mead and took five-week holidays in the summer to recharge between raids on Irish monasteries.

And while we're at it, their helmets weren't decorated with horns either. We're not allowed to keep anything fun, are we?

But if lagom's Norse origins are in fact bogus, they do at least contain a nugget of truth about the culture that spawned the myth. In this particular case, it shows how important the idea of equitable distribution is to the Swedes. So much so that we want to believe that it started with robbers and mercenaries a thousand years ago.

"Not that all linguistically unique words contain such lofty or poetic dimensions: the Scottish tartle describes the anxiety you feel when you realise you've forgotten the name of the person you are talking to."

In fact, the word originated much later; the earliest known citation is from 1637. The phrase stems not from the word "lag" as in "band" or team, as the Viking story would have us believe, but from the other meaning of the Swedish word "lag", which is "law", ie, the sense of what is right and proper.

"Lagom" therefore was an expression that urged compliance with prevailing rules – another Swedish fixation as it happens. Not one of our hipper and more rebellious sides, but there you go. Lagom's more modern and slippery meaning, that which is neither too much nor too little, has evolved over time and made the word unique, internationally.

Or is it? According to etymological dictionares, the word actually exists in Norwegian, in the forms lugum and lugom. This lugum has a more precise meaning, "appropriate, fitting, well-built, hearty." And then in step the Japanese, offering their version of something strongly reminiscent of lagom: choudo ii.

So, if you want to be pedantic about it, the word lagom is not completely, 100% Swedish. Only moderately unique. Without overstating its own specialness in any unnecessarily forceful or rude manner. You know where this is going. Lagom is, to coin a phrase, lagom unique.

There are, of course, plenty of unique words in other languages too. In German, just as in Swedish, it is acceptable to stick words together to create new, strangely precise meanings. Waldeseinsamkeit is one famous example: the special feeling of melancholy or introspection that can occur when you are alone in the forest. The Spanish sobremesa denotes the time spent at the table after eating, when you just hang out and talk.

Not that all linguistically unique words contain such lofty or poetic dimensions: the Scottish tartle describes the anxiety you feel when you realise you've forgotten the name of the person you are talking to.

Every language can boast its own inventive and original words worth exporting. What is special about "lagom" is its prominent place in its native culture, much more than, the equally Swedish word "ombudsman", which has made its way around the world and refers to a representative of civic interests vis-à-vis the government.

Even though lagom may seem abstract and a little woolly, for those trying to establish themselves in Swedish society for the first time, lagom soon becomes a very big deal. In 2016 the English-language online newspaper *The Local* interviewed Laras Pinji, who four years earlier had moved with her husband to Sweden from Dubai and started looking for a job. In the end, she sent out hundreds of applications but without any success, and often not even an answer.

"But the question remains: Is lagom a comforting 'good enough' or a restrictive straitjacket? The answer is that it can be both."

She eventually found a Swedish mentor who taught her to write a Swedish job application and CV. It shouldn't be too long, but not excessively short either. No exaggerations or irrelevancies. It must be objective, but a personal tone is a plus – within reasonable limits.

Armed with her new CV, she was soon called for ten interviews and now has a permanent job.

"The process could have been way quicker if I'd known from the beginning the meaning of lagom: that is, adequate and sufficient; not too little, and never too much."

This gives us a glimpse of the underside of the lagom cult in Sweden. It can lead to a certain timidity and stiffness, both at work and privately. "Lagom fun" is a Swedish expression that really means "not fun at all". Boring in other words. To an anxious soul, "lagom" might mean to never, under any circumstances, put anything at risk.

As lagom has been on the rise internationally, some Swedes have started voicing their skepticism. Is this really something we need to export?

My answer to that question is yes, of course. After the phenomenal successes abroad of Nordic noir – that is, violent dystopian depictions of Scandinavia as a rain-drenched hell populated exclusively by serial killers, paedophiles and their victims – it may be useful to offer a alternate view, if nothing else.

But the question remains: Is lagom a comforting "good enough" or a restrictive straitjacket? The answer is that it can be both. Words are living, changing things, and lagom is gaining new meanings, for example in the context of environmentalism.

Put in a broader perspective, lagom should never be a compulsion or an obstacle. That would be, all things considered, a completely unnecessary exaggeration.

Lagom, of all things, should always be taken with a pinch of, well, lagom.

Unique words around the world

KUMMERSPECK

German for the extra weight you gain from comfort eating. Literally, grief bacon. Why doesn't every language in the world have a word for this?

Example: The divorce was bad enough, but now I have my Kummerspeck to worry about!

HOPPÍPOLLA

The delightful Icelandic verb for jumping in puddles. Which is pretty much a year-round activity in the Scandinavian countries, according to the Tourist Board.

Example: Hurray, it's spring/summer/autumn/winter! We can hoppípolla all day long!

TSUNDOKU

A Japanese word for the condition of collecting books but never reading them.

Example: My tsundoku pile is getting so big I can't open the door to my study.

GEZELLIG

Dutch for cozy, friendly, welcoming and comfortable. Mysig as we say in Swedish, or add a few cushions and a modern lamp or two and you have Danish hygge.

Example: A spot of genever on a canal boat would be very gezellig on an evening like this.

GIGIL

This is what Filipinos call the impulse you feel to pinch or squeeze a cute child, puppy or other unbearably adorable individual.

Example: Those cheeks are so scrumptious, they are giving me a gigil rush.

WELTSCHMERZ

German again, of course. This time, it's the pain felt at the state of the world and the way people treat each other, usually felt by the young.

Example: Please sir, I would be more than happy to take part in today's gymnastics lesson, but sadly I am currently overwhelmed by my Weltschmerz.

TREND EXTRA! TOMORROW'S FASHIONABLE LINGO, TODAY

Be the first to start a fashion with these unique Scandinavian words that may very well be exported one day. Or in this case, the next wave of incomprehensible Swedish words you hardly knew existed. Use them wisely.

LAPPSJUKA

Literally: Lap-disease

The melancholy or straight-out panic felt when alone in a deserted place. This used to be considered quite common among southerners who moved to Lapland in northern Sweden.

Example: I wouldn't mind working from home if it weren't for that darn lappsjuka!

SAMBO

Literally: Co-hab

Used as a noun, this refers to the person with whom one is living, but not married. Started in the 1970s as a bit of a joke due to its also being a Swedish name, "Have you met my Sambo?" But now it's taken on a legal meaning, sambo rights according to Sambo Law.

Example: "Fancy coming over for dinner on Saturday? My sambo makes a mean fondue."

SOLOCHVÅRARE

Literally: A sun and spring man

A solochvårare is a cheat who seduces women or men and then steals their money.

"Sun and spring" is historical in origin: it was the signature famed fraudster Karl Vesterberg used in a personal ad that was answered by Miss Helga Berggren in 1916. Vesterberg stole 2000 Swedish crowns from her and ended up behind bars. Sweden's other most famous "sun and spring man" was Gustaf Raskenstam, who stole money from hundreds of single women during the 1940s.

Example: The solochvårare left behind a trail of broken hearts and bank accounts.

GÖKOTTA

Literally: Cuckoo daybreak

A wander through nature early on a spring morning. That is, around the time the cuckoo awakes and begins to call.

Example: "Fine morning for a gökotta."

RESFEBER

Literally: Travel fever

The nervous feeling you get before going travelling, for example while packing. Or before you start packing. Or as you buy the tickets. Or when you think you've lost your passport.

Example: "Three weeks before the plane takes off and I'm already down with resfeber!"

SMULTRONSTÄLLE

Literally: Wild strawberry place

A smultronställe is a spot in the woods where delicious wild berries grow. A positive place that you keep returning to, often a favourite location in general. One of Ingmar Bergman's first classics was actually called *Wild Strawberries* (1957), *Smultronstället* in Swedish. The professor, played by Ingmar Bergman's great idol, film director Victor Sjöström, revisits meaningful places from his earlier life.

Example: "This beach is my own secret smultronställe!"

FULSNYGG

Literally: Ugly pretty.

Unattractive, but in an attractive way. In practice, this really means "someone who is unconventionally good-looking". Two classic examples from the Sixties: Jean-Paul Belmondo and Barbara Streisand. Perhaps a somewhat coarser Scandinavian equivalent of that subtle, mysteriously continental... je ne sais quoi?

Example: "In the right light, I'm at least fulsnygg. You have to give me that."

CHAPTER 4

LAGOM
FOOD

Every year, between 5 and 6 million semla buns are eaten on Shrove Tuesday alone and 40–60 million throughout the semla "season". On Shrove Tuesday 2017, 56% of all Swedes planned to eat a semla. 75% prefer a classic semla with almond paste and whipped cream.

Among those who wanted to try the more creative versions Princess Cake semla came out on top, followed by the Danish pastry semla and the semla wrap, but you can also find lingonberry semla, chocolate semla and saffron semla.

Lagom Food

The Swedish National Food Agency website is devoted to exactly the kind of general information about food that you would expect from a public authority; nutritional recommendations for young and old, pregnant women and allergy sufferers, warnings about the dangers of salt and the types of fish that should be eaten only in moderation. Those kinds of things.

And then there's a somewhat hidden part, contained in a box. A question that made me do a double take when I saw that which conceals beneath its outward simplicity what amounts to the depths of despair. A question that at these latitudes could be regarded as eternal, Swedish cuisine's existential equivalent of "to be or not to be?"

The headline consists of four words. "Eat lagom – but how?"

How, indeed? The question rumbles out over the Nordic tundra. How does one go about eating neither too much nor too little? Is it possible to avoid diseases of affluence, take care of the planet and yet not always go a little bit hungry for the rest of one's life? These are big questions.

The National Food Agency's answer is straightforward and sensible. They recommend the "plate method", that is, to divide your dish into one-quarter protein, one-quarter carbohydrates and half vegetables. Ta da! It's that easy. According to qualified government dietitians.

And yet Swedes don't eat lagom any more than the rest of the McDonald's-munching, Pepsi-guzzling western world. The polarisation in the fields of religion and ideology has long been present when it comes to food in the Land of Lagom. The health freaks on one side, the crisp-eating fast food junkies on the other.

"The polarisation in the fields of religion and ideology has long been present when it comes to food in the Land of Lagom."

Traditional Swedish cuisine isn't exactly characterized by moderation. At least the ideal was never moderate. But in old peasant Sweden, people were frugal because food was too expensive to be wasted. This only made holidays and high days even more important. In the nineteenth century, the idealised Christmas banquet evoked images of barbaric Viking feasts, assuming they were in fact barbaric. Contemporary descriptions are frustratingly vague.

Literature has given us many descriptions of Christmas dinners, none more beloved for us Swedes than the one in Astrid Lindgren's *Emil of Lönneberga*. Her portrayal of a table groaning under the weight of delights in a southern Swedish farmhouse kitchen is almost operatic in its intensity.

"There, on the table, sat a plate of potato dumplings, a plate of sausages, a plate of head cheese, a plate of liver pâté, a plate of smoked sausage, a plate of meatballs, a plate of veal chops, a plate of spare ribs, a plate of white pudding, a plate of potato and pork sausages, a plate of herring salad, a plate of salted ox tongue, a plate of hacke sausages, a large plate with the Christmas ham, a large plate with the Christmas cheese, a plate with a loaf of bread, a plate with syrup bread, a plate of best rye bread, a jug of juniper cordial, a pitcher of milk, a deep bowl of rice pudding, a tray of curd cake, a dish of prunes, a plate of apple cake, a bowl of whipped cream, a bowl of strawberry jam, a bowl of ginger pears ... "

Lindgren finishes the food orgy with "a small roasted suckling pig decorated with icing." Yum, I'll have some of that with an after dinner mint.

It should be added that Emil hijacks the whole grotesque feast and gives it to the paupers in the poorhouse. No better time than Christmas to learn about the progressive politics of redistribution – a lagom Swedish attitude to Christian festivities and un-lagom overindulgence.

No modern Christmas dinner in Sweden is as exhaustive as the one in *Emil of Lönneberga*. But it is still held up as an embodiment of real Christmas. Something to strive for – except if it were actually achieved, it would burst stomachs as well as wallets.

The Swedish Christmas dinner is in fact just a festive version of the classic smorgasbord, another one of those uniquely Swedish words.

We could say that smorgasbord is just another word for buffet, but that would mean closing our eyes to linguistic nuance. A buffet is a selection of dishes, but to be worthy of the name smor-

gasbord, it has to be something else, something bigger. Maybe even mythological? A cornucopia made real? Or the Viking boar Särimner in Vallhalla that was slaughtered every afternoon only to resurrect miraculously the next morning? Talk about sustainable.

It is possible in theory to try just a little of everything, or just a few items, and go away lagom full. But in practice, a smorgasbord feast is more of an IKEA affair: build your own heart attack!

"Lent doesn't involve frugality either, strange as that might seem. In fact, this is when the super sweet calorie bomb is dropped: the semla."

Every celebration is an excuse to eat a little more than normal. Another unique food word to go along with the international hit "fika" is "kräftskiva" ("crayfish party"). Imagine a fika, but with shellfish, funny paper hats and inordinate quantities of snaps and you're almost there.

Lent doesn't involve frugality either, strange as that might seem. In fact, this is when the super sweet calorie bomb is dropped: the semla.

The semla is a sugary, cardamom bun that is cut in two, filled with almond paste and cream and sprinkled with icing sugar. The Swedes, possibly the world's most secular people, strictly adhere to the principle that it can be eaten only between Christmas and Easter.

King Adolf Frederick (who reigned in 1757-1771) would be long-forgotten if he hadn't died after scoffing too many semla buns. This fact alone earns him undying respect among modern Swedes. The fact that Adolf Frederick's last meal has been so meticulously detailed by contemporary historians is in itself telling. Apparently it consisted of smoked herring, Russian caviar, lobster, sauerkraut and boiled meat with turnips. The whole thing was washed down with champagne and finished off with semla buns, and the consequences were fatal.

The dishes with the longest history are often associated with particular festivals. Lusse buns, which are served with coffee or milk during Advent and Christmas have their origins in the pre-Christian Viking era. Their scroll shape is reminiscent of the looping dragons often carved into rune stones.

Otherwise, Swedish cuisine of the past consisted pretty much of one thing: herring, herring and more herring.

Olaus Magnus, the papal envoy, described sixteenth century herring fishing in his *History of the Nordic Peoples* of 1555. Catches were so plentiful that they broke nets. You had only to randomly plunge a spear into the water and it would stand upright by itself. And Olaus Magnus, who apparently wasn't big on fact-checking, claimed it was possible to walk across a shoal for several kilometres without getting your feet wet.

Herring is, to this day, a beloved national dish, but for centuries it was considered poor man's food. Over the course of a long winter, four out of five meals consisted of dried herring.

The first real Swedish cookbook, *Guide to Housekeeping for Young Ladies*, was published in 1755 by Cajsa Warg. The most familiar quotation from the book has almost become a saying in

Swedish: "Use what you have." Unfortunately, she didn't actually write it, but the sheer popularity of the misquotation reveals her reputation as cheerfully enterprising.

A phrase that often appears in Warg's book, however, is "if you have it." Use what you have in the larder, leftovers in other words. A timeless piece of advice and a lagom approach to sustainability.

Food in Sweden has long been characterized by limitations, imposed by both climate and the economy. Everyone had to be frugal, even those with means.

The bulging smorgasbord evolved out of the humbler brännvinsbord (literally "snaps table") of the early eighteenth century. It consisted of just salted herring – always the herring! – and, more importantly, a bottle of something stronger. The men would restore themselves with a glass, or rather a glass and a half, before the meal. "A whole" or "a half" with a piece of herring's tail. Sadly, the wives were expected to go without. Let's hope some of them had the good sense to hide a hip flask in their skirts.

Industrialisation took off at the end of the nineteenth century as the mines and forests of the north started sending money down south. This was the age that gave birth to the smorgasbord. Modest versions appeared in railway station restaurants, the perfect quick fix while you were waiting for your connection.

Then came the fridges and fast food joints of the booming twentieth century and even the middle classes were stuffing themselves like nineteenth century robber barons. This was also when the modern concept of "fika", a sweet afternoon snack, originated. A Swedish afternoon tea you might say, but with coffee. And a cinnamon or cardamom bun. And biscuits, lots and lots of biscuits. Tradition stipulates seven different kinds, a kind of smorgasbord of baked goods sprinkled with sugar rather than cold cuts.

No one would call seven different types of biscuits lagom anymore, but it was standard in 1930. These days a fika usually consists of one bun, maybe a cheese sandwich or biscuit. A lagom snack.

"Swedish cuisine sits like a misshapen, oversized suit on the dainty, proper little national soul."

Generally speaking, the Swedish taste for sweet things has gone in the opposite direction, that is, off the charts. We used to talk about a "Saturday treat", a little paper bag of goodies once a week for the little ones. But nowadays, every little cornershop seems to have a selection of sweets sold by weight, whole walls covered by them – a vertical smorgasbord of confectionary.

As early as the 1960s, the Swedish authorities realised people needed more information about food and nutrition, and so in 1965 the legendary "food wheel" was launched by the National Food Agency. Seven different categories were established: fruit & berries, fish & meat etc. The idea was to eat something out of every category every day and voilà, a lagom balanced diet.

But was the result really that lagom? If butter carries equal weight to salad, it can seem like a gauntlet has been thrown down. Equal portions of butter and salad are certainly not lagom, for either your caloric intake or your monthly outgoings. Back to the drawing board!

The National Food Agency later went with a more budget-friendly "food pyramid", bread and milk at the base and fish and meat at the apex. These days, it's all about the "plate method", but no doubt we'll get some new diagram in the future. It's not easy being lagom.

It makes business sense, however, to sell food that hankers after the Swedish love of lagom but simultaneously manages not to be healthy. Butter with only a lagom amount of salt was launched in the 1970s; then came the beloved "medium milk", which achieved the lagom, and to Swedes almost holy, balance between full fat and skimmed. So healthy in fact that you may as well have that bin bag full of sweets at the weekend.

More recently, the lagom trend has taken on a new cause: being lagom for the environment too. What would a lagom menu look like then? Eat according to the seasons! Make pack lunches during the week! Use up those leftovers! A bit like a revived Cajsa Warg, the way Swedes used to eat long ago – when not in celebration mode, of course.

But most people don't eat that way nowadays. We Swedes are pretty excessive when it comes to food, no matter how many charts are thrown at us. And maybe it's not such a bad thing in the long run. Because our national sweet tooth has given us sumptuous baked goods like fluffy cardamom buns and melt-in-the-mouth raspberry thumbprint cookies, weekday luxuries that can only be described as heavenly.

Lagom, however, they are not. Or healthy. Just like cream sauce with meatballs. Swedish cuisine sits like a misshapen, oversized suit on the dainty, proper little national soul.

The whole contradiction is personified by that absurd and most Swedish of all baked goods. You've guessed it, the semla. So sweet, so delicious – and also utterly bad for you. So completely unnecessary.

Like I said: eat lagom, but how?

To semla, or not to semla?

No, semla isn't a verb. Still, the answer has to be, semla. But semla lagom.

THE SECRET TO LAGOM SWEDISH MEATBALLS ...

The secret is that there is more than one secret. Here they all are!

1. Make them small. Really small, bite-sized balls of yum. It's a pain to roll them one by one, so forget that. The solution: A piping bag. Cuts preparation time by half, if not more.

2. Make them in the oven. It takes ages to fry a kilo of mince divided into small balls. Brown them quickly then finish in the oven. Or freeze them down and only fry however many you need at a time.

3. Meatballs need accompaniments. In Swedish restaurants those are mostly mashed potato, lingonberry jam, cream sauce and pickled cucumber. The latter two are optional, but without the potatoes and especially the jam, we're a long way from lagom. Lingonberry jam is available at your nearest IKEA, or in a pinch, can be substituted with cranberry.

Lagom Meatballs. Serves 4

400g beef mince	75 ml milk	½ onion
1 egg	75 ml cream	1 tbsp butter
4 tbsp bread- crumbs	1 tsp salt	½ tablespoon liquid beef stock
	1 pinch ground black pepper	

Mix together the breadcrumbs, egg, salt and pepper with the milk and let it sit for a while. Cut the half onion in two. Grate one piece and put it aside, then chop the remaining onion and sweat it without letting it go brown. Mix everything together until smooth.

Form the mixture into balls, with a piping bag if you have one. If you use your hands, wet them first.

Fry the balls in butter or margarine at medium heat. Once brown, turn the heat to low and continue cooking for another five minutes, or if you are making a large batch, do this in the oven.

THE SECRET TO LAGOM CINNAMON BUNS

The secret is twofold and applicable to sweet doughs in general, that is even lagom classics like saffron and cardamom buns. Firstly, be absurdly exacting with the liquid ingredients. They must be body temperature, 37 degrees Celsius, otherwise the buns will turn out stunted and not the majestic, puffed-up monuments to fika that you and your guests deserve.

Secondly, and perhaps less obviously: be stingy with the flour when kneading the second time. It's not much fun; the dough is sticky and difficult to work with and you will despair. Add a little flour if all hope is lost. But if you can hold off, your reward will come in the oven: succulent delicacies. Cracked, dry buns are an utter abomination and bring shame on any fika spread.

Lagom cinnamon buns. Makes 40–50

Dough:	Filling:	To decorate:
150g melted butter	150g butter	1 egg
500ml milk	100g caster sugar	nib sugar
50g yeast	1 tbsp cinnamon	
50g caster sugar		
1tsp salt		
800 to 850 g of flour		

Mix the butter and milk. Warm to 37 degrees Celsius and stir in the yeast. Add sugar and salt, then add the flour and knead thoroughly into a smooth dough. Cover and allow to rise for around 30 minutes. Knead the dough on a lightly floured surface and then split into two. Roll one into a long, flat rectangle.

For the filling: roll out the butter and place over the dough. Sprinkle the sugar and cinnamon on top and roll into a long sausage. Cut into discs, place into paper casings and arrange on a baking tray. Do the same with the second batch of dough. Cover with a cloth and let them rise for 30 minutes. Meanwhile, preheat the oven to 250 degrees Celsius.

Brush with a beaten egg and decorate with the nib sugar. Bake for 8–10 minutes. Let them cool on a wire rack, covered by a cloth.

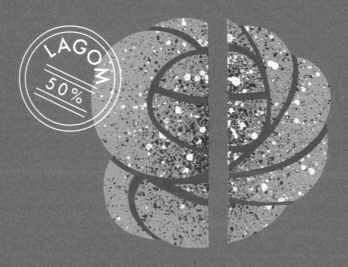

We Swedes love our cakes and buns – we average half a bun per day.

Four out of 5 Swedes follow a diet and 1 in 10 is a vegetarian.

A classic of Swedish food writing, *Swedish Cakes and Cookies*, has sold over 3.8 million copies since it was first published in 1945, making it the best-selling Swedish book after the Bible and Book of Psalms.

Swedes average 20 kilos of cheese per year – making us the biggest consumers of hard cheese in the world.

THE SECRET TO LAGOM SWEDISH BISCUITS

The secret is always to make double batches. Yes, always. They don't last long, trust me.

Märta's sliced chocolate biscuits. Makes 60

200g margarine or butter	1 tsp baking powder	To decorate:
250g caster sugar	1 tbsp vanilla icing sugar	1 egg
250g flour	1 egg	nib sugar
4 tbsp cocoa powder		

Heat the oven to 200 degrees Celsius, or 175 degrees in a fan-assisted oven. Mix all the ingredients well and split into 6 equal pieces. Roll into sausages. Place them on a baking tray that has either been greased or lined with baking paper, and flatten a little. Brush with beaten egg and sprinkle with nib sugar. Bake in the middle of the oven for approximately 15 minutes. Then, while still warm, cut on a slant into 2 cm pieces.

LAGOM FIKA

The Swedish "fika" has become trendy in recent years, but we're not going to let the hipsters keep it for themselves. Part of the very charm of fika is that it is just as much the preserve of bored teenagers as little old ladies. To hang out for hours in cafés talking all for the price of a coffee and a bun – that is the very essence of fika.

LAGOM CRAYFISH PARTY

Legendary Swedish biologist Carl Linnaeus was allergic to shellfish and classified crayfish under "insects". No one can be right all the time. Swedes today are more enthusiastic about these crustaceans, consuming 4,500 tons a year, mostly in the month of August.

Weather permitting, the Crayfish Party (or perhaps dinner, depending on the number of guests) is held outside. The timing is due to an old law – until 1994, fishing of crayfish could only start from the second Wednesday in August.

Partygoers wear colourful paper hats; no one knows why. Cheese pie for starters, then endless cracking shells as the feast begins. A song before every "skål" (or "cheers"), preferably in rhyme and a little bit risqué. These drinking songs get progressively louder and more incoherent as the night goes on. Think children's party. With lots of snaps.

These unique, if not down right absurd, items can be found in almost every lagom Swedish kitchen.

Kalle's caviar

A sandwich filling that rouses strong feelings. It's as loved by Swedes as hated by any tourist foolhardy enough to try it. In that regard, but only that one, it's a bit like British Marmite.

"Caviar" may cause some misconceptions: Sturgeon eggs are the last thing that will be on your mind as this salty sweet, light pink paste is squeezed out over your breakfast. Fun fact: the boy on the cover, who has been in place since 1953, is called Kalle in real life.

Bullen's beer sausage

An odd remnant of the last century: popular actor and gastronomist Erik "Bullen" Berglund sold his name and stern gaze to the food industry and, in his heyday, adorned a series of 30 products, from smoked herring to pork knuckles. Bullen died in 1963 and today only the sausages remain.

Lingonberry jam

In my childhood home, lingonberry jam accompanied nearly every meal including pork chops. Lingonberry goes with most things – somewhere right now, some trendy chef is combining it with pasta. I promise.

Berries are a serious issue in Sweden, especially in the north. The lingonberry is widespread in our forests, nutritious and particularly hardy. It also contains large amounts of the natural preservative pectin. Jam, juice, freeze and cook to your heart's content. The lingonberry can take it!

O'boy

A Swedish version of instant cocoa powder and yet another breakfast favourite. This product, unlike Kalle's caviar, is popular even with non-Swedes. O'boy was also launched in flavours such as strawberry and blueberry, but they soon disappeared from the shelves.

Raketost (literally "Rocket Cheese")

It hasn't been available since the mid 1970s, but this colourful soft cheese still lives on in the collective memory as a symbol of the optimism of the 1950s, when it was launched. Attempts have been made to bring it back, but the packaging is too unhygienic. The past is dirty.

Surströmming (literally sour herring)

This is perhaps the most difficult of all Swedish dishes, for Swedes as well as foreign visitors. Jars of fermented – or, to the detractors, "rotten"– herring is eaten on Swedish flatbread. The combination is called a "klämma", literally "vice" or "clamp". The flavour is powerful and salty, but the problem is the pickling liquid. It doesn't just smell, it stinks. Again, this is according to the detractors who regard it as a crime against one's taste buds, but also one's neighbours.

CHAPTER 5

LAGOM
DESIGN

IKEA's Billy bookcase first went on sale in 1979 and 41 million of them have been sold since. Designer: Gillis Lundgren.

IKEA stands for Ingvar Kamprad Elmtaryd Agunnaryd. The founder, Ingvar Kamprad, grew up in Elmtaryd in Agunnaryd parish.

The IKEA catalogue is published in over 30 languages and has a readership of 217 million worldwide.

Lagom Design

The Moomins, a family of pudgy trolls who live in a fairytale valley in the Gulf of Bothnia is, strictly-speaking, Finnish; Tove Jansson, who wrote and illustrated the Moomin books, lived in Helsinki. But she wrote the stories in Swedish, which encourages us pushy Swedes to claim ownership, at least in part.

In one episode of the cartoon series, the family becomes famous and stinking rich. How do they use the money? Remodelling their house with the latest in luxury interior design, of course. Enter the uncompromising designer, who dramatically announces that the Moomin home will be transformed into "cauliflower white with mousy-grey spots." At this point Moominmamma is, understandably, gripped by panic. In the end she and the family move into the basement, where the old upholstered and gilded furniture has been retired.

The series is a perfect condensation of the Nordic approach to design and modernity, interest in all that is delicately tasteful, but also our cautiousness. Pardon me, could I please have some creature comforts with all the cauliflower whites and mousy greys? Is there any room for mys and hygge?

In Sweden, and Denmark, and Finland for that matter, good design is a source of national pride. Names like Jacobsen, Aalto and even IKEA have stormed the world. And yet, sometimes all you want is to enjoy a hot mug of tea or coffee while sitting on a brown corduroy corner sofa. That may be a little problematic if you want to keep up with the latest trends – which Swedish people do as a rule, seizing every opportunity to throw out the old and buy the new.

This tension has always been a feature of Swedish design. Folk styles, such as the peasant paintings of the 1600s and 1700s, were characterized by colour and pattern, while prestige architects and arbiters of taste like Nicodemus Tessin the Younger – who designed Stockholm Castle – stuck to international influences more strictly. Completely contrasting aesthetics, but both examples of what we still regard as "good taste" today.

Later, Swedish designers continued to make something unique out of international trends. The most influential Swedish home of all time, that of painter Carl Larsson and his wife Karin at the Lilla Hyttnäs farm in Sundborn, was clearly influenced by William Morris's Arts and Crafts movement, and the Nordic version of the 1920s Art Deco is known today as Swedish Grace.

But it was in the 1920s and 1930s that the lagom revolution in design occurred. Swedish designers and architects became obsessed with the idea of practical homes for ordinary people. But at first they were so well-made and of such quality that their target consumers often couldn't afford them. IKEA changed all that.

Modern Swedish design, especially furniture and textiles, is a high-profile export that is surprisingly popular at home. The cliché would be an object that is both practical and somewhat strict, maybe in bent birch or untreated pine. This is not too far from the truth, and it will come as no surprise that Swedish homes generally adapt to the mass-produced, practical IKEA minimalist aesthetic.

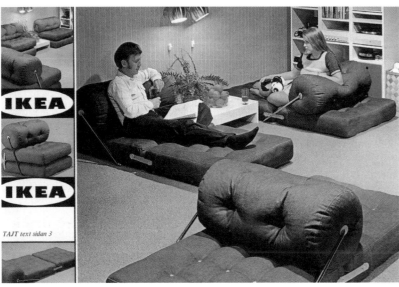

TAJT text sidan 3

Simplicity and harmony are ideals worth pursuing, but it can get out of hand. You are sure to be astounded by the variety of tastes on display in Swedish real estate adverts. Not! It's the same white walls, smooth grey cabinets and discreetly curved taps in every kitchen. Minimalism is one thing, but such cold, hard austerity is another. A little splash of colour wouldn't hurt!

On the other hand, one feature of lagom is distinctly not universal. It builds on balance, that's true, but it's up to you to find the equilibrium suitable to you – or in the case of taps, to your sink. Let one hundred lagom bloom!

There is, therefore, something comforting about the history of Nordic design. Indeed, Swedish furniture, ceramics and architecture of the twentieth century are most often characterized by a benign, perhaps sometimes exaggeratedly clever "functionalism", in which form is inexorably adapted to its purpose. And yet, that can be the source of its beauty, and sometimes even of eccentricity and fun.

In the early 1940s, potter and design legend Wilhelm Kåge churned out his delicious, lagom practical and 100% stackable plates "Grey Stripes", for decades the serving dishes of choice in school cafeterias and hospital canteens up and down the country. And yet, he also created dragon puppies.

"Outrageously expensive, Asian-inspired little ceramic dragons that look like Japanese manga figures, but decades before manga reached the western world."

"Dragon puppies?!" I hear you ask. Yes. Outrageously expensive, Asian-inspired little ceramic dragons that look like Japanese manga figures, but decades before manga reached the western world. A dragon puppy is cute but a little nasty, a sterile pet guaranteed suitable for those with allergies. Nobody actually needs a dragon puppy. But many of us would be happy to have one keep us company at the dining table or by the windowsill.

That and other oddities balance the sometimes stifling moderation of Scandinavian interiors. Kåge himself called the dragon puppy a "conversation piece", a little shot in the arm for the occasionally stiff Swedish dinner table, before the snaps and the pickled herring are served. The dragon puppy was always intended as a luxury item, but it shows that there has always been a little wiggle-room in the oh-so aesthetic and practical Swedish design lexicon. Leeway for a little joy.

"The cliché would be an object that is both practical and somewhat strict, maybe in bent birch or untreated pine."

The cauliflower-white-and-mouse-grey ideal lives on in Nordic décor. And why not? But in order to position oneself as truly lagom, there has to be something extra, unusual, one original accent. This doesn't necessarily have to be a dragon or a troll, however suitably Scandinavian they might feel, but we all need a little hint of madness that breathes life into that tasteful, pared-down harmony. If you don't believe me, just ask Moominmamma!

Lagom design classics

SWEDISH NEOCLASSICISM

The king of Sweden from 1771 to 1792 was the theatre freak Gustav III. He loved it so much he wanted to be on stage himself. It is somehow fitting that he was murdered in the middle of a masquerade ball: a simple assassination would have been far too quotidian and boring, at least this way he was dressed up for the drama.

His other interests included architecture and interior design, and his influence meant that important craftsmen and designers were imported to Stockholm. The king's travels to newly excavated Pompeii and his collection of antiques impressed the nobility. Suddenly, even the people of the Arctic Circle were on trend.

The Swedish version of neoclassicism was less ornate and gilded than the one on the continent, however; an adaptation to Swedish conditions both in terms of aesthetics and financial means.

To this day, Swedish furniture from the 1700s and early 1800s attracts buyers from all over the world precisely because of its restrained and contemporary feel: they are just lagom. Emphasis in these traditional furnishings was placed on natural materials, especially readily available types of wood such as birch and pine. Floors could be left untreated – but scrubbed – or painted, maybe to look like parquet.

The furniture, chairs and tables were made with straight lines and painted in bluish greys. The result was so elegant and timeless that IKEA recreated the look during the 1990s. A greater success aesthetically than financially, as it turned out: eighteenth century furniture is a craft and doesn't fit in cost-effective flat packages.

Swedish upper-class and country interiors look fabulous in the pages of a glossy magazine, almost ethereal, yet also earthy. No heavy drapes in such a dark country; a simple blind or some white tulle is more than enough. Ornamental items, like the ubiquitous candlesticks, usually have a practical function. The floors are covered with rugs made of old clothes, even in the larger farm houses.

Today, we would call this type of decoration "sustainable", but at the time this mix of the beautiful and the practical was merely common sense.

CARL AND KARIN LARSSON'S LILLA HYTTNÄS

The home of artist couple Carl and Karin Larsson, the Lilla Hyttnäs farm in Sundborn in Dalarna, is more Swedish than meatballs, pickled herring and Volvo put together. At least that's how it feels today. But when Karin decorated and Carl painted the interiors at the end of the nineteenth century, their style was regarded as bohemian, radical even.

Like all ambitious artists of the time, both Carl and Karin were schooled on the continent. They met in France and were influenced by the Impressionists. The British Arts and Crafts Movement, with its focus on the handmade and the traditional, was also making its mark internationally, and Carl and Karin are known to have read their magazine *The Studio*.

Together, Carl and Karin Larsson created their own style in which they mixed the airy Gustavian aesthetic – old, antique furniture that others often considered junk – with their own artwork, handicrafts and carvings. Karin's textiles and Carl's painted borders drew their influences from Japanese prints and rural Swedish folk art.

Carl depicted life at Lilla Hyttnäs in books such as *A Home* (1899). Soon his paintings became classics and were seen as a sort of ancient Swedish archetype. In fact, the ideal was modern, almost postmodern, in its studied but relaxed mix of styles. And the books themselves were made possible only by the new four-colour print technology. The Larsson couple were in fact surfing a new media wave when they launched themselves as the quintessential Swedish family. For Swedes nowadays, the pictures feel familiar and safe, so helplessly lagom that it is easy to forget how colourful, ornate and innovative the interiors actually are. Today's cool minimalism feels a world away from the variegated, forgiving Larsson home. Perhaps this is the time to return to Lilla Hyttnäs once again.

Stockholm City Library

SWEDISH GRACE

Art Deco flourished in the 1920s, becoming the first truly global artistic style. It embraced modernity, speed and luxury. Just like the era in which it was born, Art Deco was frenetic to the point of desperation, a design equivalent to *The Great Gatsby*. It goes without saying that the Swedish version was more subdued and, yes, lagom. "Protestant" according to one British commentator.

Again, young Swedish designers like Carl Malmsten cast their gazes back to the new classicism and were inspired by its graceful, airy feel. The furniture is particularly sought-after, and the style is found more broadly in architecture from the era, like Gunnar Asplund's temple-like Stockholm City Library. Every detail has been carefully thought out, even the smallest chair and door handle is a part of the whole.

The name Swedish Grace was coined by British art critic Philip Morton Shand at the Paris Exhibition in 1925, mostly to disparage the French stand, which he considered vulgar. The fashion only lasted the duration of the 1920s, but international antique dealers like James Harrison in New York describe Swedish Grace with phrases like "sober extravagance."

THE STOCKHOLM EXHIBITION

In 1930 the Stockholm Exhibition threw open its doors; the whole new temporary part of the city had been especially built. It was supposed to be devoted to crafts, but there were as many industrial objects and architectural exhibits. This was where functionalism, or "funkis" in Swedish, broke through. It is a simple enough philosophy: purpose determines form, all redundant decorative touches must be removed.

Author Ivar Lo-Johansson described bringing his parents to the exhibition. In one booth they viewed the "prison cell of the future", stripped back and cold. His aged parents cried: "Who would want to spend any time in there?"

Funkis became the prevailing style of architecture and design for the next few decades, and in time, the very epitome of lagom itself. But many people had difficulty accepting it back in 1930, even if functionalism managed to incorporate its share of glamour and aestheticism. Ewald Dahlskog's round pots, introduced at the exhibition, are a perfect example.

Lagom Design

BRUNO MATHSSON

Bruno Mathsson took chair design to extreme lengths, scrutinizing how humans sit from every possible angle. He would sit down in snowdrifts to study the imprint left by his body. This is easy to imagine when you sink into one of his beautiful and almost supernaturally exacting pieces of furniture.

The "Pernilla" armchair from 1943 is one of his most beloved designs with a graceful profile in layered wood. The chair was named after the well-known food writer Pernilla Thunberger. She was modern too and didn't hesitate to use time-saving, half-processed products and sauces in her recipes: cooking should only involve a lagom amount of time spent in the kitchen!

FOLKBÅTEN, THE PEOPLE'S SAILING BOAT

During the 1930s, the decade that saw functionalism and the birth of "the people's home", the Scandinavian Sailing Federation announced a contest: to design a cheap and practical sailing boat for the common man. Fifty-nine contributions were received, but none fully satisfied the requirements. A committee was convened to amalgamate them into the Nordic "people's boat".

The final team design was assembled by Tord Sundén and the folkbåt was finally launched in Gothenburg in 1942. Since 1976, it has also been manufactured in plastic. Many Swedes associate the design with the comedy movie Docking the Boat (1965), in which a bunch of particularly useless Sunday sailors crash a folkbåt in the Stockholm archipelago.

The rigour of functionalism started to relax and in 1940s United States, it became known as Swedish Modern. In Stockholm, a playful, luxurious take was sold in the Svenskt Tenn shop, a collaborative effort between the designers Josef Frank and Estrid Ericson.

Frank originally came from Austria and was influenced by Wiener Werkstätte, the design group that evolved out of the Vienna Secession. He was a man of his time, and yet balked at steel pipes and mechanics, preferring the naturalistic shapes of the Art Nouveau style: a lagom modernism!

Internationally, Frank's legacy survives in his colourful textiles, inspired by everything from jungle plants to city maps. In Sweden, his furniture designs are beloved status symbols with high resale value; traditional upper-class homes in Stockholm are often essentially Josef Frank museums.

LILLA ÅLAND

A case could be made that the spindle-back chair is the most Swedish piece of furniture of all time. Examples can be found in every kitchen across the country, in a thousand different shapes, and yet always simple and practical. But no one design is as beloved as Carl Malmsten's Lilla Åland, which has been in constant production since 1942.

Malmsten became an international household name during the Swedish Grace period and disliked functionalism's focus on mass production. He always emphasised craft. And yet, from the 1950s onwards, some of his furniture was produced industrially. The Lilla Åland chair is typical Malmsten: simple, discreet and comfortable. It was inspired by a chair he came across in Finströms Church on the island of Åland in the Baltic Sea.

STIG LINDBERG

Since the Land of Lagom had been in the grip of the strictures of functionalism for some decades, there arose a deep and urgent need for playfulness and colour. Enter Stig Lindberg, whose fabrics, ceramics, porcelain and book illustrations were pure confetti explosions. The immensely popular Lindberg designed everything from plastic piggy banks to television sets and fountains. In the 1950s especially, his work was a splash of technicolour in the grey of the post-war period. His fabrics and the beloved Berså service from the 1960s are back in production today.

MARIANNE WESTMAN

Marianne Westman was a contemporary of Stig Lindberg and became a symbol for the Swedish kitchen of the 1950s and 1960s in much the same way, especially with her Picknick dinner service which became an unbeatable success in 68 parts.

Her porcelain claimed groceries as pleasure with their caricatures of fish, vegetables and eggs. Like many other Scandinavian designers from that period, Marianne Westman reached an international audience and eventually moved to Germany to work there. Picknick has proved so timeless that it has come back into production in recent years.

Picknick

IKEA

Today, IKEA is a multinational company that distributes meatballs, mystifying instructions and furniture with names like Möckelby, Knodd and Knagglig all over the world. However, in 1956, IKEA was just a small-scale mail order company. Founder Ingvar Kamprad was having trouble fitting a small side table into the car after photographing it. But the legs could be screwed off and on... Bingo!

Suddenly, the Lövbacken was packed flat and designed to be assembled at home. A business idea was born that enabled IKEA to lower its prices to lagom.

The march towards department stores, lost screws and Billy bookcases on every continent had begun. Today, IKEA has also launched its own campaign for sustainability – "Live Lagom!"

ERICOFON, OR "THE COBRA TELEPHONE"

Nothing says the 1960s for a Swede quite like the Cobra Telephone, a perfect slice of lagom pop constructed from molded plastic. It was in fact officially called the Ericofon and was

designed in 1955 by Ralph Lysell and Gösta Thames. The Cobra was heavy as lead and definitely not suited to long conversations, but it looked so groovy!

THE STRING SHELVING SYSTEM

The people's home must, in addition to its people's boat, of course have a people's bookshelf. This simple but beautiful design came about just as the boat did, through a competition, in this case advertised by the Bonnier's People's Library imprint. Yes, the super-inclusive word "people" was very fashionable at the time.

Nisse Strinning was the winner, and nothing suited this democratic lagom project better than his String bookshelves. They were cheap and endlessly flexible: the metal ends and loose shelves could be customized for any wall, book collection or wallet.

TEN SWEDISH DESIGNERS

Ten Swedish designers (10-gruppen) was founded in 1970 to create textiles in happy, colourful and contemporary patterns that built on the work of greats such as Josef Frank and Stig Lindberg. Nowadays, IKEA owns the brand and carries on its legacy.

CHAPTER 6

LAGOM ENVIRON-MENTALISM

In 1975, Swedes recycled 60% of all waste. In 2015, 99%.

Swedes love to separate their waste, 9 out of 10 do so on a daily basis. 75% of all packaging is recycled.

58% of Swedes polled in 2017 believed it was important to use fewer plastic bags.

Lagom Environmentalism

One of my best friends, C-G, is a self-confessed skeptic when it comes to environmentalists. Note: not to environmental friendliness in general, as in taking the well-being of the planet into account and actively protecting it from pollution and destruction, etc. No, he's just skeptical towards those individuals who claim to be environmentally conscious.

I consider myself a friend, or at least sympathetic, to both the planet and the environment. When we meet, there are arguments.

"What's the big problem with people calling themselves environmentally conscious?" I ask, with a hint of impatience because we have trampled over this ground so many times that I already know his argument.

"You already know!"

You're right. C-G sounds a little bit frustrated.

"Yes, but I want to hear it again!"

"Why? This is meaningless."

"Such an important issue can never be meaningless!"

Sanctimoniousness is a trap that even the best of us can fall into, especially when it comes to the environment. Still, a risk worth taking, I think.

"Okay. The urbanite who calls himself environmentally conscious is just a hypocrite. A true environmentalist would live in a hut in the woods without electricity and collect water out of a well!"

"So there's no point of even trying?"

A leading question, admittedly. But C-G can handle it.

"No. Not really."

"So we should just give up?"

"Well ... " A hint of doubt.

"But you sort your garbage like all other Stockholmers. You fill your car with ethanol."

"Of course, I'm not a barbarian. But I would never dream of calling myself an environmentalist!"

C-G is a passionate person by Swedish standards; he rarely does things by halves. For those of us who know him, we can see that he is actually, although he refuses to admit it, a lagom environmentalist. Which is basically the only thing a sensible person can be.

To put all your focus on the environment, let's call it the "hut-in-the-forest" solution, would of course mean letting it take over your life. Absolutely fine for those who have the time and money to devote all their waking hours to the life of a holy fool, but unfortunately, that's not most of us. On the other hand, carrying on as normal and totally ignoring the problems of pollution and rising sea temperatures would be as extreme, and just plain stupid.

The environment is an area screaming out for lagom solutions. Which is lucky, considering they are many such lagom ideas and we Swedes have extensive, and one could say time-honoured, experience in this field.

"Allemansrätten" is another one of those unique Swedish

words, but it is yet to make a mark internationally. Probably because no one outside of Sweden's borders can understand this popular custom. People are allowed to roam free on private land? Build fires and even camp overnight without needing permission? Absurd. But Swedish lagom thinking is built on the idea of consideration, both to fellow citizens who might cross your land and to the landowners in turn.

Lagom commitment to the environment is also based on consideration – this time, of our entire planet. We don't want to put too much burden on Mother Earth, while at the same time, we must be allowed to live well but within our scarce resources.

"Lagom commitment to the environment is also based on consideration — this time, of our entire planet."

Again: Swedes are very aware of these limits. Nowadays, Sweden is a rich, industrialized and materially prosperous country, but most of our history has been characterized by long winters, erratic summers and an insecure supply of food.

As we all know, the Vikings took long journeys across the globe for the simple reason that the resources at home were so meagre. The forests of pine and fir in northern Sweden became economically valuable only in the nineteenth century.

In that kind of environment, you learn to save but hopefully without being mean, because nobody likes that, not even Swedes. And you learn to reuse stuff instead of throwing it away, some-

rationella
hjälpmedel
för
hushållet

ICA

thing that in practice is just as much a matter of imagination. If nothing else, this is evidenced by all the beautifully preserved rag rugs and patchwork quilts that still fill Swedish homes, a folk craftsmanship practised for centuries.

Of course, this behaviour wasn't called "sustainable" back then, even if that was exactly what it was. So sustainable, in fact, that it's more relevant today than ever before.

Swedish people's lagom thinking has fluctuated over the years, however. The 1950s happened here too. That is, the decade that gave us young stars like James Dean, Elvis Presley and Marilyn Monroe, and an explosion in pop culture. Consumerism may not have been invented in the 1950s, but that was when it morphed into the epic dream that took over the entire western world, a plastic flower that blossomed in the ruins of World War II.

Everything had to be big, and preferably American, in the 1950s: cars, breasts, furniture. Not exactly a lagom attitude, but Sweden caught the bug too.

All the gadgets that were suddenly available! Technical progress and a booming economy led to the spread of washing machines, refrigerators, coffee makers, vacuum cleaners and, most of all, the fabulous television with its accompanying "TV flasks" (thermos flasks filled with coffee), "TV tables", "TV trays" and "TV dinners".

These new fashions weren't just for the rich as they had been before – they were available to everyone, or at least to the many. Shopping seemingly without limit. And of course there was an endless supply of energy to drive all of these electricity-guzzling miracles. "Our Friend the Atom" didn't just defend democracy in the form of nuclear weapons, it also worked for everyone's well-being in safe, ultra-modern nuclear power plants!

A typical expression of the 1950s: "ultra". "Modern" was no longer enough. "Ultra" or "super" was the order of the day. The opposite of lagom.

The whole attitude towards technology and development became an almost fanatical trust in the future, bordering on a denial of history. After experiencing two world wars, the Great Depression, fascist dictatorships and, finally, the atom bomb, people in the 1950s were not interested in nostalgia. Everyone looked forward. Whatever happened couldn't possibly be worse than what humanity had just suffered through.

But it was exactly this uncritical attitude towards technological development, as well as to the hegemony of the West, that led us to the present-day environmental crises. We have only just begun trying to clean up after the frenzied consumer orgy that began in the 1950s. Many of our most acute environmental problems, which the "sustainable lifestyle" is attempting to solve, have their roots in that time. Some examples:

• Nuclear power was devised as a permanent solution to our energy problems. Securing nuclear power plants against possible meltdown was considered so uneconomical that it became impossible in practice. But what did that matter? They were considered infallible.

• Poisonous DDT was spread on fields throughout the world in a commendable attempt to combat malaria mosquitos, but the result was widespread environmental disaster.

• The 'balance of terror', a mathematically exact system for East and West to match each other's military strength that in fact prompted the defence budgets of the superpowers to explode.

Absurd numbers of nuclear weapons were stuffed into mountain bunkers and submarines.

• Consumerism became a way of life and the constant hunger for new goods led to the throw-away culture that has resulted in mountains of waste and successive natural disasters.

The world got a taste of the sobering backlash to this consumerist hysteria as early as 1962. Rachel Carson's ground-breaking book, *Silent Spring*, revealed the DDT scandal and served as a wake-up call to the modern-day environmental movement.

Today, half a century later, it is clear that humanity has to work together to ensure that the Earth's resources are enough for all. And yet, humanity is also occupied elsewhere. With work, family life, social media and television binges. We can't all move to the forest.

It is in this spirit that we should take onboard the environmental tips outlined in this book. It would be exhausting to follow every single one to the letter. But if each of us does at least something, it won't require some of us to do everything. What matters here, as in life in general, is a lagom effort. Maybe even ultra-lagom.

12 ENVIRONMENTAL TIPS FOR THE HOME

1. Switch to **energy-efficient bulbs**, especially those that last will be kept on for a long time.
2. **Recycling** is easy peasy, and efficient at that: a recycled aluminium can takes 95% less energy to manufacture than a new one. The energy saved by recycling a plastic PET bottle corresponds to 33 hours of burn-time for an 11 watt energy-efficient bulb.
3. **Lower the indoor temperature** a degree or two. It makes a difference! Then put on a warm sweater.
4. **Make do and mend.** Learn from our frugal ancestors; don't automatically buy new gadgets all the time. Clothes can be patched, furniture fixed. Your smartphone will last a few more years if you change the battery.
5. **Buy sustainably.** There is now organic labelling, such as the EU Eco-label, for everything from food to stationery.
6. **Change your electricity provider** if you can. Make sure the energy comes from sun, wind or water – and absolutely not fossil fuels.
7. **Don't set up home in your shower.** Heating up water guzzles energy. Take short and effective showers, or maybe even cold ones? They have the added benefit of being fast!
8. **Install solar panels** on the roof if you own your own house. It takes a few years to make good on the investment, but solar energy is becoming more efficient and cheaper all the time.
9. **Give potted plants as presents.** Cut flowers are often doused in chemicals and transported long distances by air, all for just a few days of pleasure.
10. **Avoid plastic.** Plastic is made mostly of natural gas and crude oil, and it should be noted that PVC plastic (marked 3 and with a triangle) can interfere with the body's hormones, cause cancer and even reproductive problems. Buy natural materials like glass and wood instead.
11. **Buy secondhand.** Recycling of old gadgets is always good for the environment, and when buying secondhand, you often get something unique, or at least unusual.

12. **Things that can be washed and reused are better than disposable ones.** Wipe up sniffles with a cotton handkerchief just like Grandpa used to, and save wood and energy!

5 ENVIRONMENTAL TIPS FOR TRAVEL

1. **Car-share.** You can either co-ordinate with friends and neighbours, join a not-for-profit car pool or buy membership in a profit-making company. The result is the same: fewer fossil fuels consumed – and you'll save money on petrol, parking, insurance and maintenance. Ka-ching!
2. **Avoid airplanes.** For short, domestic travel especially. Air travel affects the environment most negatively during take-off and landing, so short and repeated flights are particularly harmful.
3. **Go by train** instead of car and plane. The environmentally friendly way to travel with zero fossil fuel emissions! And super relaxing. Suggested reading: *Murder on the Orient Express*. Pretend the murder victim was a dumper of radioactive waste.
4. **Get on your bike.** The environment will thank you for it, as will your body.
5. **Check your tyre pressures.** An easy way to reduce both environmental impact and costs if you own a car. Properly pumped tyres demand less juice and last longer.

In 2013, Swedes recycled 150 tonnes – the equivalent to 15 Eiffel Towers – of electrical waste, lamps and batteries: four times the EU target. (Source: Rekoguiden)

7 TIPS FOR THE LAGOM ENVIRONMENTAL ACTIVIST

1. **Exert pressure on your elected officials.** Your impact on the Paris Agreement might be limited, but you can do a lot at the local level. You can influence plans for new buildings being built nearby, the exploitation of natural areas and waste management more than you might think. Municipal documents are open to the public, easy to check, and politicians are sensitive to opinion. Call, email – get yourself noticed!

2. **Read up.** Politicians are stressed out. If you find out all the facts about a single issue, you will often become more knowledgeable on the topic than your elected representative. Take advantage of this. And you can easily organise friends and friends of friends.

3. **Social media.** Start a specific group for your project. Together you can influence political decisions. Make sure you post something new at least a couple of times a week, even if it's short. The page has to feel alive.

4. **Fact check.** "Facts" easily shared on social media almost always reflect the views of the poster. If the claims are shocking, be sceptical. Where do the numbers come from? How were they chosen? Are they current? Try to go back to the source and then share what you find.

5. **Old media.** Local newspapers and radio are constantly looking for news about your neighbourhood. Throw them a bone by organising resistance to a suspect building development, and then give them a call.

6. **Don't be provoked.** There's nothing like environmental issues to get passions going, yours included I imagine. Internet trolls will find your page. But keep your cool, be polite and stick to the facts. Oh, and block accounts that spread lies and hatred.

7. **Have fun and be fun.** Keep in mind that funny images or video clips are immensely popular online. Earnestness and dedication can sometimes be expressed in the form of a joke – and go viral.

BECOME A RECYCLING SUPERSTAR

Recycling may not be brain surgery, but it's not always that straightforward either. Some simple principles to keep in mind:

- **The packet trick.** Some crisp packets, for example, are considered metal, others plastic. How do you know the difference? Scrunch the packet in your hand. If it bounces back: plastic. If it remains in a ball: metal.
- **Paper bags.** It's easy to believe that paper bags belong with newspapers, but actually, they should be sorted as cardboard!
- **Glass and metal** are almost indestructible and can be reused an infinite number of times, provided they are actually collected. If they end up dumped in nature, they are broken down very slowly (300 years for an aluminium can) or not at all and can cause considerable long-term damage.

LAGOM SWEDISH ENVIRONMENTAL MILESTONES

1941 The book *Alarm Clock* by Elin Wägner. Feminist and ecologist Wägner was roundly criticised for this groundbreaking book when it came out. Today we know she was just ahead of her time in the way she connected peace, environmental protection and maternity.

1970 *Moneybags on the Bog* by Annika Elmqvist. A real Swedish children's classic, this is a story about an evil capitalist who is constantly polluting the environment in some way or another. Moneybags wears his top hat and suit even when doing his "business" on the toilet: "he sat down to deliver, and out it ran into the river."

1971 *The Apple Wars* by Hans Alfredson and Tage Danielsson. Beloved satire in the form of a fairy tale. Trolls and imps get their own back on investors who want to attract tourists to a Nordic "Deutschnyland."

2008 *Silent Seas* by Isabella Lövin. With her depiction of the catastrophic situation for the world's fish stocks, Lövin shook the Swedish fishing industry. She is currently Sweden's Deputy Prime Minister and Minister for the Environment.

Today Ikea goes lagom! In 2016, Ikea launched its "Live Lagom" project, which encourages sustainable lifestyles. The company also aims to produce as much renewable energy as it consumes by 2020.

7 ENVIRONMENTAL TIPS FOR THE GARDEN

1. **Natural pesticides** are now easy to find if your plants need them.
2. **Sprinkle with rainwater** as much as possible. And do it in the evening. During the day, most of the water evaporates instantly, wasting water, not to mention your energy too.
3. **Compost more.** It's worth your while to turn a corner of your garden into a compost heap where you can recycle food waste, eggshells, coffee grounds and other organic matter. But check first that it's allowed where you live.
4. **Fertilize the vegetable plot with manure** such as from horses or chickens, or else compost or seaweed. But be careful not to overdo it; any surplus will be washed into nearby lakes by the rain.
5. When you buy **garden furniture,** "hardwood" almost always means tropical in origin. Check that furniture is stamped with the Forest Stewardship Council (FSC) logo. This ensures that it isn't coming from rainforest and contributing to deforestation, but from socially and economically sustainable sources.
6. Switch to **solar-powered outdoor lamps,** which work just as well on the balcony in town.
7. **Lawnmowers** should be manual, unless you have a big area to cover, in which case opt for an electric lawnmower. And if you must have one with a petrol motor, go for alkylate fuel as it's kinder on both you and the environment.

CHAPTER 7

10 KG

0 Kg

LAGOM
FASHION

During the 1950s, import restrictions were in place in Sweden which was great for local jeans manufacturers such as Algots. They were lifted in 1960, however, and American brands such as Lee and Levi's started to dominate.

In the 70s, Swedish brand Gul & Blå became popular and young people queued outside the flagship store in Stockholm to get their hands on a pair of V-shaped jeans. Their biggest success came with the TT model. Desperate mothers had to call ahead and order pairs because their children refused to go school without them. At the height of their success, Gul & Blå made 100,000 pairs a year at their factory in the village of Vegby.

Today's big Swedish jeans brand, Acne, was founded in 1996. The name stands for Ambition to Create Novel Expressions and you can find their clothes all over the world, from New York to Tokyo.

Lagom Fashion

And now, time to cast a grenade at established fashion history: Coco Chanel was Swedish!

At least, that has to be the conclusion. How else do we explain the clothes and perfume designer's famous words: "Some people think luxury is the opposite of poverty. It is not. It is the opposite of vulgarity."

Pretty lagom, huh? Think about it. If some archeological team of the future should ever excavate a tablet carved with the Ten Commandments of Lagom, rest assured, Chanel's pronouncement will be on it. Near the top.

A simple, well-designed, forgiving – and expensive – item like Chanel's little black dress can, in its own way, be taken as an example of lagom. In terms of taste, definitely lagom. No excess there. But maybe also financially, at least if you think about it in terms of a 25-year investment. A well-made item of clothing can last for decades, as does a classic silhouette.

And yet, we Swedes can't lay claim to the grande dame of the fashion industry. Partly because she is most definitely French, an inconvenient fact in itself, but also because she lived most of her life staying at a hotel. A dream for many, including the author of this book, but clearly a complete extravagance and therefore most definitely not lagom.

And yet Coco Chanel and her wise words embody this paradox at the heart of the fashion industry. Haute couture and seasonal changes in fashion personify flightiness, hyper-consumption and excess – and yet as an industry it is also driven by supply and demand, sustainability and craftsmanship, desire and profitability.

Which brings us to Mah-jong, a Swedish clothing brand that in its day became a kind of political marker, at one point the height of nostalgic kitsch, and now ultimate classic. This is itself a kind of sustainability – to be able to refashion one's symbolic meaning along with the changing times. The way we see fashion moves in discernible ways.

Mah-jong was founded in 1966 and stayed in business for a dramatic ten years. Mah-jong's clothes became a symbol of the student movement and the social upheavals of the early 1970s, a uniform of sorts for the radical wing of the youth movement in Sweden.

The clothes themselves were provocative and a little odd: unisex, and in the early years colourful and daring in their patterns – they were sold even on Carnaby Street during London's swinging heyday. The name itself was a statement of solidarity with socialist China.

The models in the catalogues were friends and children of the designers in everyday outdoor milieus. Mah-jong suits were made from soft materials such as plush, corduroy and silk tricot, and were in sizes to fit all ages, genders and body shapes. Unisex was all the rage at the end of the 1960s, and it lived on in the brand's slouchy overalls of the 1970s.

Much of the thinking behind the clothes feels surprising even

today and yet anything but extreme: the clothes weren't made in sweatshops in the Third World but right here in Sweden, and they weren't seasonal. The collection was built around a base wardrobe that was supposed to last for years – lagom for the environment as well as the wallet. Although, it must be added that this was in the long-run as these weren't cheap clothes in the H&M vein.

During the 1980s of Margaret Thatcher and Ronald Reagan came the inevitable backlash against the left. Swedes love consensus: in the 1970s it was fashionable to be lagom politically engaged, and ten years later it was lagom amusing to make fun of the ideological wave that by that time had ebbed away. Mah-jong found itself in the firing line, especially their unisex overalls. "Mjukismannen" ("The Plush Man") became an It phrase of the period, referring to the velvety material of choice. It wasn't meant as a compliment.

And yet, Mah-Jong's clothes were sewn to last. They command high prices at vintage shops these days – both the early, colourful stuff as well as the 70s more understated monochrome designs. Those who kept their Mah-Jong pieces now have to fight off their daughters and granddaughters to wear them.

Should you want to find Mah-jong's polar opposite, H&M would be an obvious candidate. Inexpensive, conventional garments that are made to be replaced and sewn on the other side of the world. And for those who might be wondering about the company's name, there is absolutely none of that socialist unisex stuff here, thank you very much. H&M is an abbreviation of Hennes & Mauritz, the female and male departments respectively. The divisions are clear-cut.

But there are also similarities between the two brands. Both H&M and Mah-Jong brought fashion to the people, with commercial insight in one case and ideological in the other. Both revolted against the norms of the previous generation: functional and forever-mended clothing for people with limited resources.

The first incarnation of H&M, which back then was merely Hennes, opened in 1947. Founder Erling Persson made a trip to the United States and discovered clothing stores with a broad range of items at reasonable prices built on fast sales. Hm, lagom pricing, could that work in Sweden? Indeed it could. Hennes was an instant success.

"The clothes themselves were provocative and a little odd: unisex, and in the early years colourful and daring in their patterns – they were sold even on Carnaby Street during London's swinging heyday."

But during its first decades, H&M was painfully uncool, a clothing company but not a fashion company. It was only in the 1970s that H&M began to attract the young, trend-conscious consumer. Or lagom trend-conscious, perhaps. H&M is not one of the true innovators of fashion in Sweden. And just like IKEA furniture, their designs could almost be mistaken for those of more established designers – almost – as H&M started to be obviously

"inspired" by its more famous competitors. Copies, but at a fraction of the price. A recipe for success that holds as true today as ever.

In recent years, as H&M has garnered international success with its exclusive collections, produced in conjunction with fashion designers such as Karl Lagerfeld and Stella McCartney. Good for both publicity and status, no doubt. But the basic idea is still the same as in 1947: large amounts of clothing sold cheaply and fast.

There were precursors to both H&M and Mah-jong in Sweden, even many decades earlier. One such example, founded in 1886 by radical writer and aesthete Ellen Key, was called the Dress Reform Society. A solemn name, but isn't all successful fashion a kind of clothing reform in a way?

The reform, or revolution, for which they argued so passionately was for clothes designed according to the body's natural shape. Just like Mah-jong. No uncomfortable bustles in the back that made it impossible to sit comfortably, no corsets that distorted the rib cage and made it difficult to breathe. At that time this was a radical idea.

The Dress Reform Society never became a commercial success; maybe its liberal ideas were before its time. At the beginning of the century, the Swedish fashion industry consisted of fancy ateliers for the rich and famous, like the legendary Augusta Lundin Studio and luxury department store NK's "French" tailors. Both carefully copied the spring and autumn trends from Paris, just like H&M would so many years later. But for the fashion enthusiasts without a fat trust fund to fall back on, these couture houses were out of reach. For them, it was all about patterns, sewing machine, needle and thread.

Swedish fashion during the first half of the twentieth century wasn't much to cheer about either. A younger look barely existed: childhood ceased when you finished school and a lagom Swedish girl turned into a little old lady, at least in appearance.

The great Swedish breakthrough in fashion would have to wait until the post-war period of the 1950s, with the creation of the "teenager" and the cult of youth in popular culture.

Teenagers had existed before of course, as did generational conflict. Middle-aged tabloid journalists decried the young "jazz boys" daily in the 1930s, and by the 1940s there had even been youth riots in Kungsträdgården in Stockholm. But it was in the 1950s that the age group was taken seriously by the fashion and film industries, and that made all the difference. This was the beginning of the shift from the 50-year-old to the 16-year-old as the ultimate fashion icon.

This resulted in whole new ways of combining cloth, colour and pattern. Young designers like Gunilla Pontén and Kerstin Lokrantz exploited new materials like denim and modeled their own clothes. Fashion illustrator and journalist Kerstin Thorvall contributed advice and assistance to create a new world of fashion writing in magazines and books.

During the same period, Katja of Sweden – or Katja Geiger as she's really called – made her international breakthrough. Her clothes were simple, almost minimalistic. She said that she wanted them to look good when sitting in a scaled-back piece of Bruno Mathsson furniture. At the same time, her designs were the epitome of lagom: practical, but just fancy enough for a party too.

This has remained the ideal in Sweden to this day. Everyone wants to dress lagom well, something that looks good at work and an evening on the town without being too formal. Because that would be a mortal sin.

But then came the fabulous and unfettered 1970s, a challenging time for all this lagom. Not to mention the fact that 1972 saw a real Swedish fashion milestone: the launch of "Alla stjärtars byxor", literally "All Bums' Pants". The name happens to sound like the Swedish for Valentine's Day while also being another cry for equality: All bums made equal! All bums united! No bum left out in the cold!

"But could those soft bums really handle such tight jeans?"

This wasn't the only example of Swedish advertising's remarkable obsession with the derrière in the 1970s. A campaign for Lilla Edet toilet paper consisted of a full-page advert of a little boy dressed in a sailor's outfit sitting on an outdoor lavatory, itself a loaded symbol in Sweden that evokes the freedom of summers spent outdoors. The slogan: Even tough boys have soft bums.

But could those soft bums really handle such tight jeans? The question was taken very seriously in the Land of Lagom. By the mid-1970s, super tight flared jeans were all the rage across the globe and were met with an outcry by the Swedish press – expensive, restrictive, could anything be more aggressively anti-lagom? Swedish clothes had never been so uncomfortable and close-fitting. Even their health implications were extensively researched, including how their tightness might negatively affect sperm count.

"By the mid 1970s, super tight flared jeans were all the rage across the globe and were met with an outcry by the Swedish press – expensive, restrictive, could anything be more aggressively anti-lagom?"

But if you were to ask anyone outside Sweden to say what came to mind when they heard the phrase "Swedish clothes" in the 1970s, the answer would probably be the glam stage outfits worn by ABBA. Those glittery platform shoes were unforgettable and quite possibly unforgivable. They crossed all boundaries of good taste and even the laws of gravity.

Platform shoes were very much a part of that era and made it even to my childhood home of Umeå, 600 km north of Stockholm. Though rarely as boots and more often as platform clogs, a classic lagom solution; cutting-edge glamour remade for the humdrum of the everyday.

I wore flares in the 1970s but never platform shoes, not even of the clog variety. I confined myself to what we in Sweden call näbbstövlar, literally "beak boots". The word is pretty unique. They were inspired by Sami folk styles and came to a little point at the toe. They were as important a part of the leftie uniform as a

Palestinian scarf, round glasses or Fjällräven jackets.

Fjällräven is a Swedish sport and leisure brand that has, absurdly enough, quietly taken over the world in the last few years – their Kånken rucksacks have even been sighted around the private schools of Manhattan's Upper East Side. Just how strange this seems to my generation of Swedes cannot be overstated.

The Swedish fashion industry is a force to be reckoned with on the global stage: not only H&M but also Acne and Odd Molly. Swedish designers are known for their interpretations of the lagom ideal. Clothing by designers such as Anna Holtblad, Lars Wallin, Filippa K and Nygårds Anna can be colourful or discreet, but never stiff or uncomfortable. The common thread is rather their body-loving and tasteful shapes that are anything but ostentatious.

This restrained, even subdued, good taste is a selling point, but also a limitation. Let's just say that there's a reason that the British television classic about fashion victims Patsy and Edina is called *Absolutely Fabulous* and not *Absolutely Lagom*. Edina, in an unforgettable performance by Jennifer Saunders, rages around in extreme, mismatched high fashion outfits by bat crazy continental designers like Christian Lacroix and Jean-Paul Gaultier. "Lacroix, sweetie!!" is her classic battle cry when anyone questions her taste.

"This restrained, even subdued, good taste is a selling point, but also a limitation."

What can I say? "Nygårds Anna, sweetie!!" just doesn't have the same schwing.

Of course, Edina and her PR friend don't seem to give two hoots about the impact of all this on the world and nature. The Swedish clothing industry, in contrast, has had a collective environmental policy in place for years, and H&M advertise that they aim to be an "environmentally positive" company by 2040 at the latest.

Can it be true? Even throwaway H&M have jumped on the sustainable bandwagon and taken on the modern version of lagom. While at the same time realising Coco Chanel and Mah-jong's ancient truth: a practical and handsome item of clothing should withstand trend cycles just as well as washing cycles for years to come.

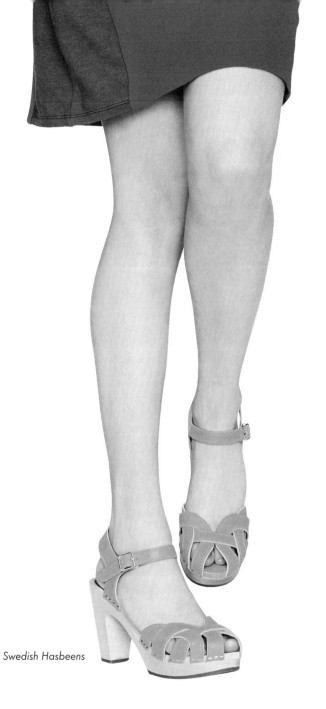

Swedish Hasbeens

JEANS

Too much
Nothing wrong with denim. Of course. But the scariest fashion lessons learned in the 1970s still hold today: NO THANKS to floor-length denim skirts, denim coats, denim vests, denim umbrellas and above all else, denim caps.

Too little?
Nothing wrong with ripped jeans, but don't take it too far. Or else a pair of much-loved ripped jeans could end up protecting your legs as much – or as little – as a pair of fishnet tights. Good for catching colds though.

Lagom!
501s of course. You can't get more classic than a pair of those. And preferably a bit worn. Lagom worn.

SHOULDER PADS

Too much
According to conventional historical explanations, shoulder pads are evidence of the militarisation of women's fashion and are especially popular during times of crisis, such as the 1940s.

Too little?
A total lack of shoulders, not just shoulder pads.

Lagom!
Shoulder pads are back, but not too much, for winter 2017. Is this an omen? War? Depression? Considering how understated they appear to be in this latest incarnation, hopefully only a minor recession.

638-530

Too much

Platform shoes make a comeback every few years – exactly why remains a mystery. One advantage to wearing these monsters on your feet: they force you to slow down. Maybe they could be rebranded as Mindfulness Boots?

Too little?

Great for dancing en point, ballet flats do less well in the rough and tumble of every day life. Not quite as irrational as platform shoes, though. And they looked good on Audrey Hepburn in the ultra-feminine 1950s.

Lagom!

Sneakers. There is nothing more lagom than a shoe that performs just as well on a jog as a day at work.

ACCESSORIES

Too much

Pets. We can blame Paris Hilton for the horrible, seemingly immortal "match-your-Chihuahua-to-your-sunglasses" trend. Cats in Versace necklaces are just as bad. Let me be clear on this: pets should not be reduced to the status of accessories and fashion details should never be able to pee and poop. There, I said it.

Too little

Chanel No 5. Nope, perfume is not an item of clothing, whatever Marilyn Monroe said. Nor is it an accessory. It's just lazy! Why make things so complicated? See below.

Lagom!

The classic handbag. Now we're getting somewhere. A well-chosen bag doesn't just look good but is also practical. Why not a classic Palmgrens in rattan? Steal one from your Swedish relative.

COLOURS

Too much

Clothes made from flags. Traditional folk dress is dubious except on rare occasions, but any clothing – that in-cludes hats, shirts, dresses and suits – made from flags are an abomination. Even at football matches.

Too little

White jeans. On a beautiful summer's day, fine. Otherwise, no!

Lagom!

Scarf. A splash of colour around your head or neck works whatever the weather. And if not, it's easily removed.

CHAPTER 8

LAGOM
GLOBAL

GLOBAL GAMING MIRACLE

These days, the Swedish games industry can give pop music a run for its money as a global export. The Battlefield series has alone sold 60 million copies and has a legion of devoted fans around the world. Not to mention Minecraft, one of the most influential games ever.

Lagom Global

Swedes have a reputation for being reserved and cold, but we love to travel, are obsessed with communication and leave our mark. We send our pop music, tennis players, film stars, supermodels, depressed police detectives and flexible shelving systems out over an unsuspecting world.

It all began a thousand years ago, in the early Middle Ages, back in the days when an average European moved about ten miles over the course of a lifetime. Nordic people wrote with runes, and about half of the six thousand that have been preserved are in Sweden. The rest have achieved an impressive geographical spread, especially given the primitive communications of the 900s A.D. Viking script has been found from as far afield as Newfoundland in the west to the Caspian Sea in the east. Runes are even carved into the balustrade of the Hagia Sophia Mosque – a former Cathedral in Istanbul, former Constantinople. This was how bored Scandinavian mercenaries passed the time during long masses.

All this is to illustrate what we may wish to call the global lagom paradox: given how moderate and self-effacing we Swedes happily consider ourselves to be, we are still quite international.

As builders of empire, Scandinavians are nothing to write home about. Viking settlements in Greenland, Britain and Rus-

sia soon collapsed, were conquered or just assimilated with the locals. Later, in the seventeenth century, Gustavus Adolphus's attempt to make Sweden into Northern Europe's great Protestant superpower was short-lived. Germany and Poland remain German and Polish.

Maintaining colonies requires considerable quantities of manpower and stamina. Never mind the perfectly legitimate moral objections, suppressing entire countries for generation after generation is no lagom task.

So we Swedes move instead. It is no coincidence that the closest thing to a Swedish national epic is Vilhelm Moberg's trilogy *The Emigrants* about the hardships faced by poor Swedish farmers moving to America.

In 2017, around one hundred thousand Swedes lived in London, or as some enthusiasts call it, "Sweden's third city." This is of course not the case: London would in fact be Sweden's ninth largest city, after Helsingborg but before Linköping. Still, not bad!

According to similar figures, São Paulo in Brazil in the early 2000s was, somewhat unexpectedly, Sweden's largest industrial city, populated by the employees of large companies such as Scania, Astra Zeneca and ABB.

We Swedes like getting out in the world, we just can't stop ourselves. And once there, we are rarely humble, spreading our lagom philosophy, sometimes passive-aggressively, sometimes just aggressively.

"All this is to illustrate what we may wish to call the global lagom paradox: given how moderate and self-effacing we Swedes happily consider ourselves to be, we are still quite international."

Gustavus Adolphus's daughter, the scandalous Queen Christina, is a good example. She imported intellectual trends, and on occasion the intellectuals themselves, to Stockholm, including the greatest philosopher of the age – Descartes, the "I think, therefore I am" guy.

He didn't last long in the damp, badly heated Castle of Three Crowns, however, and died of pneumonia after just a few months. The early mornings – Christina was an advocate of 5 am philosophy lessons – may have been the cause. "Sweden's lone contribution to international philosophy," according to malicious commentators. But what do we care? We have ABBA and IKEA!

When Christina then converted to Catholicism, she immediately moved to Rome in order to take part in energetic and stimulating arguments with multiple popes. I like to think she fired off a few "This is how we do it in Sweden," but in Latin.

It should surprise no one that three hundred years earlier, it was a Swedish saint, Bridget, who badgered the pope of the day Urban V. He lived in exile in Avignon, not in the holy city of Rome, of which Bridget strongly disapproved. Everything in its place! In 1999, Saint Bridget was promoted by John Paul II. Now no ordinary saint, but patrona Europae. It pays to speak out.

This is a tradition with deep roots: a small country with a notoriously modest and inhibited population – that is also more than happy to tell the world's most powerful men how to act.

During the twentieth century, for example, Dag Hammarskjöld acted as the second Secretary-General of the UN, and Prime Minister Olof Palme agitated against the United States invasion of Vietnam and Franco's Fascist regime in Spain. Hans Blix, a Swedish UN weapons inspector, refused to find any sign of weapons of mass destruction in Iraq in 2003, despite the demands of the United States.

There is something strange about the intensity of Swedish interest in the outside world. Perhaps it's because we are aware that we live in a small country and speak an insignificant language. We want to be noticed, despite our reputation for being provincial and sheepish. And yet every time we actually succeed, we're surprised.

It would look bad to take success for granted. Not lagom. But we gulp the recognition down once it appears, and never it let go. Who invented the wrench for example? A Swede. Who designed the first Coca-Cola bottle? Again, a Swede. The zipper? I'll give you three guesses.

This is an essential part of the Swedish national character, which is otherwise quite vague and mostly confined to longing for a red cottage by the sea.

The Swedish national day is 6 June, but few know why it falls on this date and even fewer actually celebrate it. I can reveal exclusively that it was the day Gustav Vasa was elected King in 1523 and the country got a new constitution in 1809. There you go, facts that evade over half of all Swedes!

While we don't care about anniversaries, we do care about Swedish success abroad. Which brings us to a phenomenon that hardly anyone else in the world cares about, but that we Swedes have turned into an obsession. We call it the Swedish Miracle.

"But that's how we look at it: if someone abroad wants to listen to Swedish pop or read a Swedish thriller, it's a miracle, something that can and should be considered equal to, say, rocks that turn to bread or burning bushes that speak."

Miracle in this instance is not, as you might think, something like hot water in the middle of winter, but Swedish export successes of all kinds. Journalists always call them the Swedish Miracle: The Swedish music miracle, the Swedish tennis miracle and so on.

One might think that "miracle" has a funny religious ring to it given the context. But that's how we look at it: if someone abroad wants to listen to Swedish pop or read a Swedish thriller, it's a miracle, something that can and should be considered equal to, say, rocks that turn to bread or burning bushes that speak.

In a suitably lagom way, it is a clear example of the contradictory Swedish traits of modesty and megalomania. Modesty because any international interest in us sad and grey Swedes must be considered odd. But also megalomania because we - every one of us! - see ourselves as part of this miracle.

What was the first Swedish Miracle? Perhaps some of the earliest movies of the 1910s. Film was an international medium in the early days when it was silent, and Sweden found itself at the forefront with filmmakers such as Victor Sjöström and Mauritz Stiller. Sjöström's *The Phantom Carriage* (1921) was an early example of the use of advanced special effects, the *Avatar* or *Jurassic Park* of its day.

The first modern Swedish Miracle came in the 1970s in the form of the Tennis Miracle led by Björn Borg, Mats Wilander and Stefan Edberg, who dominated the top ranks for a decade.

Then came the Music Miracle at the beginning of the 1990s when bands like Ace of Base and the Cardigans were regular features on the newly launched MTV Europe. The wave hasn't receded, as dance music artists such as Swedish House Mafia, Avicii and Robyn and singers such as Lykke Li and Zara Larsson continue to do well.

The Swedish Crime Novel Miracle seems to be just as hardy, with Stieg Larsson, Henning Mankell and Åsa Larsson delivering a regular supply of blonde corpses and police detectives. Some hopeful souls have even written about the Fashion Miracle, mostly due to H&M and Acne. In 2007, jeans overtook vodka for the first time as the leading Swedish export. Absolut cheers to that!

In recent years, the Swedish press has started laying claim to a Food Miracle. Swedish and Danish chefs are making names for themselves internationally with gourmet organic food, often with a side of moss, bark and twigs. The Age of the Miracle is clearly still upon us.

There is something a little irritating about the whole thing. Isn't it enough that we have to keep hearing about these Scandinavians lavishing in their generous social welfare and nicely designed houses, do we have to buy their jeans and eat their moss and lichen as well?

When Donald Trump attacks Sweden by passing on falsehoods and misunderstandings about riots and terror attacks the whole world takes note, precisely because the image of Swedish is so goody-two-shoes and seemingly perfect.

Of course, Sweden is not some hellish inferno with "no-go zones", but neither is it a paradise where everyone agrees and sick pay falls like manna from heaven. The truth is far more lagom.

We Swedes read and discuss how we are portrayed abroad, usually via our screens. Because above all else, we love digital technology. Free and functioning Wi-Fi, even on the metro. Which is why it's rather fitting that one of the most widely used IT technologies is named after the old Viking king Harald Bluetooth.

Bluetooth was invented by engineer Jim Kardach. He happened to have read a translation of the Swedish classic adventure story *The Long Ships* and fell for the name. Now every smartphone, speaker, camera, remote control, fridge, electric key and all the other thousands of gadgets that use Bluetooth technology are inscribed with the symbol made up of the runes for H and B.

Those old runes again. They continue their travels.

Swedes have a tendency to make a name for themselves out in the wider world. But they also usually keep their feet on the ground, which is much appreciated back home in the Land of Lagom.

Swedish blonde bombshells

With all due respect to vodka and IKEA, Sweden's most famous exports have typically been models and film stars.

ANITA EKBERG

Anita Ekberg became Miss Sweden in 1951 and was drawn to Hollywood, where her overwhelming blondness scored her roles opposite comedians such as Bob Hope and Abbot and Costello. But it took Federico Fellini's casting of Ekberg in *La Dolce Vita* in 1960 for her star to really rise.

Fellini expert Tullio Kezich on Ekberg: "A real workhorse. She threw herself into the Trevi Fountain, which was icy cold, without hesitation or complaint. Marcello Mastroianni was scared of getting a cold."

ALEXANDER SKARSGÅRD

Alexander Skarsgård belongs to an entire acting dynasty. His father Stellan is famed for his roles in films such as *Thor* and *Breaking the Waves*. Alexander got his breakthrough as the alluring vampire Eric Northman in the series *True Blood* and has gone on to play everything from the title role in *The Legend of Tarzan* to a wife-beater in *Big Little Lies*.

BRITT EKLAND

Britt Ekland was a staple of the international gossip columns of the 1960s and 1970s, the archetypal Swedish blonde: actress, celebrity wife, model and exercise fanatic. She starred in the James Bond film *The Man with the Golden Gun* (1974) but was most famous for her spectacular private life with husbands Peter Sellers and Rod Stewart. The British tabloids slavered over the contents of her scandalous autobiography *True Britt* (1980).

Refreshingly frank in interviews: "I like my wrinkles. You can't look like a smooth bun your whole life. But I will get a facelift, and it'll be fun. Then I'll tell you all what I've done."

Lagom Swedish singers

Sweden has produced a remarkable number of opera singers. Is it because it sounds like we're singing when we talk?

JENNY LIND

The big star of the nineteenth century, perhaps the most beloved opera singer of all time – Maria Callas could be her only competition. Unbelievably popular in the UK and US: she was welcomed by 30,000 cheering fans in New York harbour before she'd even sung a note. The America tour, organized by circus king P.T. Barnum, made her financially secure for the rest of her life.

She came from a poor background. The entry in the parish records states merely, "Parents unknown." Niklas Jonas Lind only claimed paternity only after she got rich.

JUSSI BJÖRLING

Probably the greatest tenor of the twentieth century, sorry Pavarotti, Domingo etc. His voice was unforgettable – lyrical, smooth, melodious. He performed at the Metropolitan in New York from 1938 until his death in 1960. His private life was a tragedy, however. Hypersensitive, he drank heavily. He was pushed hard from the age of 5 and performed with his brothers all through his childhood.

BIRGIT NILSSON

Worshipped for the force of her singing and precision of her pitch, Nilsson was born to render the works of Richard Wagner. Her unique voice earned her praise from all corners of the globe. Her irreverence and scepticism towards feared and humourless superstar conductor Herbert von Karajan became the stuff of legend.

What was her favourite role? "Isolde made me famous, Turandot made me rich." When Karajan insisted on dim, gloomy lighting for his staging of *The Ring* in 1967, she arrived at rehearsals dressed in a miner's helmet, complete with searchlight.

Lagom brands

There are a few Swedish products that have become global concepts in their own right.

DYNAMITE

Chemist Alfred Nobel invented dynamite in 1867, revolutionising explosive technology during the building boom of the late nineteenth century. Finally, the unstable and hazardous nitroglycerin could be abandoned.

To the shock of his family and the world, the childless Nobel gifted his considerable wealth to individuals who have "made the greatest difference to the world", thus creating the Nobel Prize.

VOLVO

Volvo, which is Latin for "I am rolling", was founded in 1927. Along with competitors SAAB, it symbolises the Swedish automotive industry. And in America especially, their cars became known as the brand of choice for academics and lefties. Volvo was an early adopter of safety features such as the three-point safety belt and disc brakes.

ABSOLUT

Absolut Vodka is a colourless, flavourless distilled spirit – but in some mighty sexy packaging. The original bottle was found in a pharmacy in Stockholm's Old Town. The company's advertising campaign has been one of the twentieth century's longest running and most successful, devised by American agency TWA in 1980. The slogan, "Absolut Perfection" has since had over 800 different reincarnations around the globe.

In Sweden, however, unflavoured vodka has always been a low-status drink. Cheap, domestic brands such as Explorer have long been associated with alcoholism and despair. Absolut's export success has done something at least to overturn that image.

CHAPTER 9

LAGOM
HAPPINESS

SUMMERHOUSES

Half of all Swedes over 16, that is some 4 million, have access to a summerhouse or caravan. Of these, around half are the owners. The others rent or borrow.

HOLIDAYS

Statutory holidays by country:
USA 0 days
Japan 10 days
Canada 15 days
Venezuela 15 days
Australia 20 days
Sweden 25 days
Brazil 30 days

MIDSUMMER

The song Små Grodorna ("Little Frogs") that Swedes sing when they dance around the Maypole on Midsummer's Eve is in fact a military march from the French Revolution. "Frogs" was the British nickname for the French, referring to their supposed eating habits.

Lagom Happiness

"Happiness is a warm puppy," cartoonist Charles M. Schulz declared in his series *Peanuts* in 1962. The phrase became the title of a little book that sold in the millions and was then taken up by an endless number of horrifically sentimental imitators. Coffee table books and postcards were never the same again. Schulz didn't stop at warm puppies, he also informed us that "Happiness is walking barefoot in the grass," and that "Security is a thumb and a blanket." And why not? Happiness is what you make of it.

But to actually take happiness seriously, to truly define it with scientific accuracy? A hopeless task. You would think.

And yet, all kinds of think tanks and universities are valiantly trying to make a science out of the art of measuring happiness in different countries, and believe themselves to be doing so with some success. In these circles, happiness is defined with phrases like "subjective well-being" and "life satisfaction", which fools no one. The crucial question in these surveys looks innocent enough, but is in fact quite leading: "How satisfied are you with your life?"

So what exactly do we learn from all these bar charts? Well, that Scandinavians – who, to be clear on this, live right up near or in the Arctic Circle which is drenched for most of the year in ice, rain and slush – are, contrary to all reason, happier than most. Denmark and Norway top the lists and Sweden and Iceland are chomping at their heels in the top ten.

There are reasons for us Nordic people to be satisfied with life. Most Scandinavians have a high standard of living, education and healthcare are essentially free, our governments are democratic and fairly uncorrupt.

"Scandinavians – who, to be clear on this, live right up near or in the Arctic Circle which is drenched for most of the year in ice, rain and slush – are, contrary to all reason, happier than most."

We've also been at peace for a long time, which is not an insignificant detail. At the bottom of the list of 158 nations are war-torn countries like Syria and Afghanistan.

And yet, Swedes and Scandinavians in general are known internationally for our melancholy, perhaps not entirely unreasonably. Two of our biggest cultural ambassadors in the twentieth century were the steely Greta Garbo (and her lugubrious alto in *Grand Hotel* from 1932: "I vant to beee alaaaawn!") and the legendary Björn Borg, known by his opponents as "The Iceman".

And it can't be denied that the Scandinavian cultural giants aren't exactly a cheery bunch. Danish philosopher Søren Kierkegaard gave the world existentialism, the Norwegian artist Edvard Munch did for anxiety disorder what Walt Disney did for talking ducks, and the Swedish writer August Strindberg claimed that bourgeois family life was nothing more than a man-eat-man struggle for survival.

So, anguish and misery. No wonder the world gladly buys into this image of the depressed Scandinavian. But is this image correct? The short answer is no, of course not. Every country is home to every personality type.

Even the myths aren't consistent. After those miserable men of the nineteenth century came the film stars of the twentieth century. Ingmar Bergman kept the melancholy going of course, but an equally influential counter image can be found in Vilgot Sjöman's *I Am Curious – Yellow* (1967) and its follow-up *I Am Curious – Blue*: the Swedish sin! The Danes later contributed with their version, but curiously, there never seems to have existed any Norwegian sin whatsoever.

The slightly odd image of the Swede as the frustrated, sex-crazed suicidal murderer spread across the globe. First, a good bonking, then, the rope. How did this stereotype make psychological sense? Especially as the gorgeous Swedish summer was also sold to the world in Bo Widerberg's exquisite *Elvira Madigan* (1967).

We can sum up the twentieth century's picture of the Nordic countries as follows: a delightful meadow, populated by equal parts merrily fornicating couples and bodies hanging from their homemade nooses. Maybe the lovers are taking their own lives out of exhaustion after too much intense, outdoor lovemaking?

The sex-crazed image seems to have waned in the global mind but the dark, culturally-dependent gloominess lives on. Just as the statistics show chart-topping happiness.

Maybe one depends on the other? With a naturally dark outlook on life, it doesn't take much to make us happy. Perhaps just two months of sunshine per year is enough? If we're lucky.

People sometimes talk about "the tyranny of low expectations", but maybe Nordic low expectations are actually our best friends? Or maybe not low expectations. Lagom expectations.

Here is the key. Nordic happiness isn't dramatic or revolutionary. No, it's just perfectly lagom. That's what happens when your culture and ideals were formed before the breakthrough of the welfare state.

When asked to describe happiness, the average Swede will come up with such universal values as security, love and family. But they also mention summer, sun and a place in the country. In other parts of the world, one house is good enough, but we windswept Swedes desire one more. A little one. For the summer.

This ideal was immortalised in 1940, at the peak of "the people's home" period, in a popular song: "The sun shines on little cottages too, and in that cottage I want to live with you."

Note that the dream cottage is small. The summer house is a national fantasy, but the dream is not of a castle or an estate with servants and walled gardens. No, it's a cottage. A little cottage.

The song continues: "A little garden and beautiful orchard, a little outhouse with a green heart in the door." That's right, an outdoor toilet. A lagom fantasy that doesn't even involve running water. At least, not in 1940.

Just as urban songwriter Cole Porter was revitalising Broadway with his sophisticated rhymes, Swedish popular music was tackling the big issues of running water and electricity in summer residences. And the image lives on: many Swedes still romanticise their rustic outhouses, including the leaky bucket that has to be emptied at some point. But the outhouse is certainly sustainable from an environmental point of view: free manure for the potatoes.

I can't resist citing one more line from that homey old song: "Wouldn't it be lovely to live like that, not a cent in debt to anyone!" Sanitation and financing – because in 1940 the world was at war and the Great Depression was fresh in people's minds. Happiness has to be financed.

This practical take on the joys of life is typical lagom thinking. It might seem a little goody-goody, but at least it's unpretentious, as befits the definition of lagom.

Swedes relieve the cold and gloom by sucking every last drop out of the summer months in these little summer houses, whether owned or rented. And during the rest of the year, we increase our quota of happiness with small but strategically timed celebrations of light that don't exist anywhere else. They can seem to be a little frightening to the uninitiated: the St Lucia celebrations in December are a case in point.

It all starts at 6 am when a strangely dressed blonde Swede surprises you with a sad, Italian fisherman's song and then presents you with coffee, gingerbread and some heathen saffron buns, all served with a forced smile. And she does this while balancing a crown of lit candles on her head.

Every year, Lucia is chosen in a beauty pageant without a swimsuit in sight: to celebrate a Sicilian saint who chose to poke her own eyes out rather than be forced into marriage. Her connection to Swedish Christmas is not exactly crystal clear.

The whole thing is considered most charming and a great marketing tool for Nordic culture. We can only imagine how many years it takes off the lives of the older Nobel prizewinners. Writer Isaac Bashevis Singer looked particularly jittery when he was forced to sit through the display in 1978.

These St Lucia celebrations might sound extreme, but they feel perfectly lagom to most Swedes – December certainly deserves a second festival of light, we need one more. And then in April there is Valborg with its bonfires. Midsummer is not uniquely Swedish, but I can safely say Swedes must be the only people to celebrate the longest day of the year by pretending to be frogs while jumping around a Maypole. Such extreme activities become lagom in an unforgiving climate like ours.

Lagom happiness can also take the form of cultivating what we might call complementary extremes, Sweden's two big pop culture exports: Nordic Noir and Scandipop, two sides of the same coin.

Swedish crime novels usually contain a few necessary basic ingredients, the genius psycho-killer, his many victims – often women and children – and then the detective who arrives late and is depressed. Maybe he overdosed on black coffee?

The murders are meticulously carried out – "There's a pattern," the police conclude grimly at the scene of the second crime. I used to find it irritating that so many criminals seemed to gather in one small town, Wallander's stomping ground Ystad, with corpses buried in every corner and sex slaves set on fire in every field. Or that Lisbeth Salander was so relentlessly ingenious and that her laptop was like *The Junior Woodchuck Guidebook* in Donald Duck: an oracle with all the answers.

But I was wrong. Nordic Noir describes Scandinavia in just as much detail as Bram Stoker's Dracula does Romania: that is, not at all. It's just one dark dreamscape. Which is kind of fun.

Especially when there is another force at work in the form of dance music exports Robyn, Swedish House Mafia and Avicii. Together with the psycho-killers and moody detectives of Nordic Noir, they form a whole: no light without darkness.

"We can only imagine how many years the whole thing takes off the lives of the older Nobel prizewinners."

Maybe this is why the Lucia celebrations just before the winter solstice could be the ultimate Swedish happiness symbol. Just like pop music and detective fiction, it has been shamelessly stolen from abroad and adapted to fit local conditions.

In this particular case a Sicilian saint, burned and tortured, but now decorated with candles in her hair and carrying a big plate of gingerbread and saffron buns.

Also, a thermos of coffee! Don't forget that thermos. Fika without coffee doesn't make anybody happy.

"But I was wrong. Nordic Noir describes Scandinavia in just as much detail as Bram Stoker's Dracula does Romania: that is, not at all. It's just one dark dreamscape. Which is kind of fun."

Lagom happy and sad

Nordic celebrities and culture in general tend to be known for being serious and depressing or plain silly. The truth is a lot more lagom!

EDVARD MUNCH (1863–1944)

Depressing

The Norwegian artist didn't have a fun life: his childhood was marked by the death of his mother and sister to tuberculosis and his father's "almost deranged" religious fervour. His painting *The Scream* (1893) has become a global symbol for psychological crisis and one of twenty pictures that make up the series *The Frieze of Life*.

... but fun!

Yes, Munch had a sense of humour, if somewhat caustic. He was friends with Swedish celebrity writer August Strindberg but the relationship soon soured. Strindberg was particularly displeased when Munch gave a lithographic portrait of him in 1896 the deliberately misspelt title "Stindberg" ('stind' means fat in Norwegian).

INGMAR BERGMAN (1918–2007)

Depressing

No one has done more to further the reputation of Scandinavians as chilly than world-renowned director Bergman, with titles such as *The Hour of the Wolf, Crisis* and *Shame*. Bergman himself often spoke of his tortuous anxiety about God's silence and the meaninglessness of life, but he also saw ghosts and suffered from crippling indigestion.

... but fun!

Stomach problems were dealt with in fart scenes in *Fanny and Alexander* from 1983. According to Harriet Andersson, one of his prima donnas, Bergman was incapable of telling funny stories – but his autobiography *The Magic Lantern* nevertheless contains plenty of hilarious gossip about, among other things, Laurence Olivier's dirty china plates.

GRETA GARBO (1905–1990)

Depressing

Garbo was one of the world's foremost female superstars in both silent and early spoken film. She just about always played exotic, tragic roles in which she died at the end – be it from consumption, murder or suicide – but always tragic and visually striking. Privately, she never enjoyed her fame och always fled from the press and her fans. She used to sit in silence at dinner parties. "I have nothing to say."

... but fun!

Garbo was also a competent comedic actor who could laugh at herself. Check out the romcom *Ninotchka* (1939) in which she pokes fun at her frosty image.

NORDIC NOIR

Depressing

Nordic crime novels are full of woman killers, cut up bodies and drugged children. It's pure misery, but perhaps also a little titillating that these Gothic horrors are happening to blond, well-paid Scandinavians. We deserve it!

... but fun!

Contemporary Nordic noir owes a debt to the Ed McBain-inspired couple Maj Sjöwall and Per Wahlöö who wrote about Detective Marin Beck in the 1960s and 1970s. Exciting, well-researched and garnished with comic side characters such as Constables Kristiansson and Kvant, the Swedish equivalents of Thomson and Thompson.

Lagom Happiness

ASTRID LINDGREN (1907–2002)

Happy!

All around the world, Sweden's most beloved children's author is best known for Pippi Longstocking who sleeps with her feet on the pillow, has a bag full of gold coins and is the strongest child in the world. The Russians however have a particular love for Karlsson from *Karlsson on the Roof*, a round, impudent little man with propellers on his back.

... but sad.

Less well known are Lindgren's more melancholy tales. In *The Brothers Lionheart* (1973) for example, the young hero dies in chapter one. What a typically dreary Swede! But Lindgren took her inspiration from English-language children's classics like *Seven Little Australians* by Ethel Turner and *Little Women* by Louisa May Alcott, both of which contain tear-jerking death scenes. It was the 1800s, children died! Sad but true.

INGRID BERGMAN (1915–1982)

Happy!

When the young Ingrid Bergman landed in Hollywood in 1939, she was the "natural" and unaffected starlet, in sharp contrast to the gloomy Garbo. She comes across as frank and cheery in both interviews and her autobiography.

... but sad.

Bergman's most memorable performances were always tragic, such as Ilse in *Casablanca* (1942) and the cold mother in *Autumn Sonata* (1978) in a collaboration with Ingmar Bergman (no relation). She was never that convincing in comedic roles.

ABBA

Happy!

No other pop group epitomises uncomplicated fun quite like 1970s sensations ABBA, helped by the era's absurd penchant for glitter and plat-form shoes. The musical Mamma Mia! ups this effect by adding Mediterrane-an sun, sea and sand.

... but sad.

ABBA's lyrics are surprisingly sad and pessimistic. The two couples in the group split not so long after their first major success in 1974, and "break-up" songs make up a large part of their biggest hits. Relationships are often described in terms of desperate competition: *The Winner Takes it All!* And there is always a loser. "One of us is crying, one of us is lying in her lonely bed ... "

PARTIES

Happy!

Crayfish parties, Lucia celebrations, Midsummer... Swedes seize on every opportunity to dress in strange outfits and sing cheery songs.

... but sad.

Many of these parties – especially the crayfish ones – involve hard liquor. Scandinavians, like the Russians, live in the Vodka Belt so all this fun often, if not always, runs the risk of ending up a drunken mess.

Photo Credits

P. 17: Axel Oxenstierna:
Painting by S P Tilmann,
photo: SPA, Queen
Christina: Unknown artist
/Dantesällskapet.

P. 18: Unknown photographer/
Wikimedia Commons.

P. 21: Photo: Erik Holmén.

P. 26: Unknown photographer/
Public Domain.

P. 27: Photo: kenrob/Tradera.

P. 28: Unknown photographer/
Public Domain.

P. 32: Arla/press photo.

P. 33: Toblerone/press photo.

P. 39: Illustration by Leonard
Leslie Brooke/Wikimedia
Commons.

P. 40: Photo: Karl Heinz
Hernried/The Nordic
Museum/press photo.

P. 78–79: Photo: Johnér
Bildbyrå.

P. 81: Photo: Getty Images.

P. 92: Kalles kaviar/press photo, Bullens pilsnerkorv/
press photo, lingonberry
jam: Ikea/press photo.

P. 99: Carl Larsson/Wikimedia
Commons. IKEA Cata-
logue cover 1973. © Inter
IKEA Systems B.V. 2016

P. 100: Photo: Gustavsberg/
press photo.

P. 102: Photo: Gustavsberg/
press photo.

P. 103: Illustration: © Moomin
Characters™

P. 104: Photo: Bukowskis.

P. 106: Photo: Arild Vågen/
Wikimedia Commons.

P. 107: Photo: Karl Alfred-
Schulz/Public Domain.

P. 108: Rum21/press photo.

P. 110: Svenskt Tenn/press
photo.

P. 111: Gustavsberg/press
photos.

P. 112: Gustavsberg/press
photo.

P. 114: Nisse Strinning: Olsson
& Gerthell/press photo,
"Jamaica" Birgitta Hahn/
Palett-paleteau.

P. 115: Rum21/press photo.

P. 121: Photo: Getty Images.

P. 123: Catalogue image/
ica-historien.se/.

P. 124: Photo: Getty Images.

P. 128: Carpool: University of
New Hampshire/Public
Domain, The Dandy
Horse/Public Domain,
Lawn Mower/Organics.
org/Public Domain.

P. 139: Antik & Auktion/press
photo.

P. 142: Acne Studios/press
photo.

P. 147: Fjällräven/press photo.

P. 149: Pearl Sky High,
Swedish Hasbeens/press
photo.

P. 151: Joan Crawford/Public
Domain.

P. 158: Utvandrarna/The
Emigrants, moviezine.se/
press photo.

P. 160: Olof Palme and Dag
Hammarskjöld/Wikimedia
Commons.

P. 161: Alexander Samuelsson,
unknown photographer/
swedishfreak.com.

P. 164: Björn Borg: Nationaal
Archief/Creative Com-
mons.

P. 166: Anita Ekberg: unknown
photographer/Public
Domain, Alexander
Skarsgård: Big Little Lies/
press photo.

P. 169: Birgit Nilsson: University Musical Society/
Creative Commons.

P. 171: Absolut Vodka/press
photo.

P. 185: Greta Garbo: Queen
Christina, Piano Necktie/
Public Domain.

P. 186: Ingrid Bergman,
unknown photographer/
Wikimedia Commons.